Cooking With A Spanish Flair

Published by: Instituto para la Promocion Espanola
de los Productos del Olivar (IPEPO) Madrid

President: D. Alfredo Jimenez - Millas

Director: D. Luis Patac de las Traviesas

Printed in the U.S.A. by Rand McNally & Company for
Spanish Olive Oil Institute 666 Fifth Avenue, New York, N.Y. 10019

Cooking With A Spanish Flair

CONTENTS

A special feature of this cook book is the nutritional information (calories, protein, carbohydrates, fat) accompanying most recipes. The nutritive breakdowns were prepared by Dr. Stephen Kreitzman, Nutran, Inc., P.O. Box 15464, Atlanta, Ga., 30333, based on average values. Certain recipes may vary, due to the natural variations of some of the ingredients used. The nutritional data has been figured for the complete recipe, including a sauce, dressing, dumpling when suggested as an accompaniment. Oven Baked Turkey, for example, features a Barbecue Sauce. The nutritive breakdown listed implies use of the sauce with the turkey.

Olive Oil: Nature's Gift Through the Centuries

The olive tree, you might say, is as old as time. Nobody knows just where . . . or when . . . the olive came into being, but it figured in ancient mythology and is recorded in the Bible.

Egyptian temples, more than 5,000 years ago, used olive oil for their lamps and it is in Egypt that the natural process for extracting oil from olives is said to have been first used. Interestingly, that same process is the one on which our present day methods for making olive oil are based. (See "How Olive Oil is Made," page 9.)

Some believe that the olive tree originated in Persia, while others say the Nile Valley or near the river Jordan. Regardless of the exact location, it is

To trace the beginning of olive oil one must turn to the Mediterranean Sea and surrounding lands. Egypt recorded use of olive oil more than 5,000 years ago. Exact origin of the tree is believed to have been in the Near East.

generally agreed that the olive tree came from the Near East.

From its beginnings there, the olive tree spread westward to Spain, around the Mediterranean. And each nation along the way is thought to have not only transmitted knowledge of its cultivation, but also to have added knowledge about its uses.

The Phoenicians, Greeks, Jews, Carthaginians, Romans, Arabs and Spaniards are all credited with having planted and propagated the olive tree.

The Bible makes reference to olive trees in the Old Testament, where in Judges 9, verse 7, the story is told of trees selecting a king. They turned first to the olive tree. In declining the honor, the olive tree said:

"The mission which God has conferred upon me, to the benefit of mankind, is too important for me to be able to distract my attention with the cares associated with such governance."

According to a popular Spanish legend, the olive tree goes back to Adam. On his death bed, at age 930, Adam is said to have remembered that the Lord promised him "the holy oil of mercy."

And so Adam sent his son Seth up into the mountains where Paradise on Earth was supposed to exist. Seth returned with three seeds from the deadly tree of Good and Evil, which were buried with Adam.

The seeds germinated and in a short time shoots sprang up. One became the olive tree, one a cedar

From the Near East, the olive tree spread westward to Spain, around the Mediterranean. Phoenicians, Greeks, Jews, Carthaginians, Romans, Arabs and Spaniards are all credited with having planted and grown the tree.

3

and the third, a cypress.

But, whatever its origin, the olive tree has grown abundantly along the Mediterranean Sea.

Of ancient populations, only the Assyrians and the Babylonians were not familiar with the olive and its oil. Greeks, Romans and Hebrews, on the other hand, considered it "the holy tree."

Mythology includes a story which is thought to pertain to the olive tree. In this particular tale, Jupiter has promised the territory of Attica to Neptune or Minerva, whoever gave him a gift most useful to mankind.

Neptune gave a horse, swift as the wind. Minerva gave a small branch, stating that it would become a strong tree, capable of living for centuries . . . whose produce could be eaten and whose oil could season food, sooth wounds, strengthen bodies and light the night.

Jupiter, delighted, decreed that Attica should be given to Minerva (translated Athena in Greek) and that Attica's capital should be named after her: Athens.

The olive tree was consecrated by ancient Greeks to Minerva, and this reverance of the olive was transmitted to the Romans, who gave sprigs of the olive to citizens of special merit.

Just as the tree itself was praised, so did men come to appreciate its fruit. History tells us that it was Cecrope, founder of Athens, who taught men to extract oil from the olive tree which he brought there from Egypt. Plato, Aristotle, Caesar . . . all used olive oil to season their food.

Cultivation of the olive tree in Spain dates back to the days of the Romans. In fact, Spanish ships carried oil to the Roman Empire as evidenced by heaps of clay vessels found near Rome, bearing seals of the first Spanish olive oil exporters.

S panish ships brought olive trees to the Western Hemisphere in 1560. Historians believe that knowledge of olive cultivation spread from Peru to the Antilles, Chile, Argentina, Mexico and northward to California.

Today, there are close to five million acres of olive trees throughout the world. Spain grows the largest percentage of olives (34%), with Italy next in line (30%), followed by Greece (12%), Portugal (8%), Tunisia, (6%) and Turkey (4%).

About 99% of the world's supply of olive oil is produced in countries of the Mediterranean, although some is made in California, South America and Australia.

The Bible makes reference to olive trees in the Old Testament (Judges 9:7). According to popular Spanish legend, the olive tree goes back to Adam. Mythology even includes a story pertaining to the olive tree. Spanish cultivation of the tree dates back to the days of the Romans. Spanish ships carried oil to the Roman Empire, in fact.

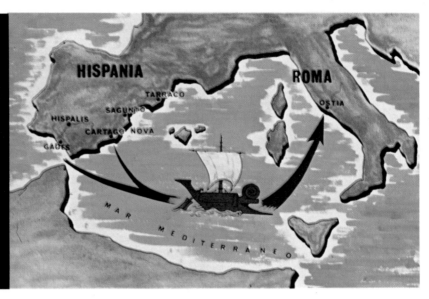

From Spain, ships sailed to the Western Hemisphere in 1560 (left) and brought olive trees with them. Cultivation spread from Peru northward to Mexico and California. Gnarled trees (right) grow close by an ancient Roman arch and symbolize the influence exerted by Romans on Spanish olive oil culture.

Just as the Romans built aqueducts in Spain (left) so did they bring with them their method of extracting oil from the olive. Today, the olive industry has grown to the point where olive crops are harvested on more than 5 million acres throughout the world. About 99% of all olive oil comes, however, from countries of the Mediterranean.

How Olive Oil is Made

From the time an olive tree is planted, it takes 25 years for it to reach maturity. But it begins to give fruit after 10 years and from that time on, olive oil can be made. While slow-growing, the olive tree has a long life. An evergreen tree — bushy and sturdy — it stands anywhere from 10 to 40 feet high. And it seems to grow in the most unpredictable, rocky locations. A grove of olive trees is a beautiful sight — with the distinctive silvery green leaves blowing in the wind.

Olive oil is the oil extracted from the fleshy part of ripened fruit. Oil makes up about 18 to 28 percent of the ripe fruit, depending on climatic conditions and care in cultivation.

An average tree gives 22 pounds of olives during harvest, yet since the tree is quite unpredictable, harvesting ranges from large quantities to nothing at all per tree.

In Spain, the world's largest olive oil producer, there are some 210 million trees and from their fruit come some 400,000 tons of olive oil each year.

Olive trees are grown mainly for their oil, although some are pickled for eating. In Spain, more than 90 percent of the olive crop is crushed annually for oil.

The flavor of olive oil depends on the variety of olives used, their ripeness when picked, the way they are handled and the length of time they are stored before pressing.

Experts believe that the best oil comes from olives picked just after ripening, before they turn black. If too green, the resulting oil often has a bitter taste; if too ripe, the oil tends to become rancid.

Rainfall is essential for good olive oil, since it improves the soil, regulating its moisture and protecting trees from weeds during the growing season.

To catch every drop of life-giving rainfall in the spring and fall, the soil is carefully cultivated . . . by tractor-driven plows in open areas and by hand near the roots of the trees. Workers can only dig down six inches or they will damage the thicker roots, cutting into the very life of the tree.

Equally important for a good olive harvest is the pruning of trees, done in winter, after the harvest, and before the sap begins to flow.

Small white flowers cover the trees in late spring, and several months later, tiny fruits (called drupes) appear. One-seeded, like cherries, they grow . . . oval-shaped . . . to lengths of about 1½ inches. These olives begin life as green fruit, and turn a deep violet by November, when harvesting begins in the more temperate areas.

It takes until January for olives to ripen in areas where the climate has not been as favorable.

Harvests are long and expensive, particularly since in spite of mechanical improvements, much of the work is still done by hand.

There are two principal methods for harvesting olives:

(1) THRESHING: branches are shaken by long poles and olives fall onto nets or sheets on the ground. Tractor attachments are also used, which

Olives, turned deep violet in color, are ready for harvesting.

"Threshing" requires branches to be shaken vigorously by long po

"Milking" by hand is one method used to remove olives from tree

8

Romans crushed olives with huge, conical-shaped stones.

Modern presses extract olive oil in much the same manner.

After pressing, filtering . . . oil is left to settle in large tanks.

grab hold of the main trunk and shake the entire tree vigorously.

(2) MILKING: workers run their hands through the branches, with fingers half open. Olives fall onto sheets or nets on the ground. Ladders are used for treetops.

In very hot summers, hail is an enemy most feared by olive growers. Because of the weather's uncertainty, it is not until the olives are actually safe within the mills that growers can be sure of their crop.

Upon arrival at the mill, olives are first weighed, then washed and ground. Olives, including pits, are coarsely crushed in various types of grinders, all developed from a principle perfected by the ancient Romans.

In those former times, huge stones (in conical and cylindrical shapes) turned slowly over lower mill stones, crushing olives and forcing oil from the fruit. A modern variation finds olives being crushed by corrugated metal rollers in brick trenches.

This is the first drawing off . . . the creation of virgin olive oil, at room temperature. A product of superior quality.

But there is a large amount of oil remaining in the pulp or mash substances. This pulp is then placed in coarsely woven fabric, folded over to make pulpy blocks known in the industry as "cheeses".

Each "cheese" is about three feet square and three inches thick. Ten or more of them are placed, one on top of the other, with slates in between. Pressure is then applied hydraulically and additional olive oil juices are collected.

This oil is filtered through woolen cloth and allowed to settle for 24 hours in funnel-shaped tanks. Sediment is drawn off at the bottom.

Afterwards, the oil goes to settling tanks, lined with glass or tin. It remains in these tanks for anywhere from two to five months, and additional sediment is drawn off at intervals.

Finally . . . the oil is ready for canning and bottling . . . and shipping eventually to continents around the world. Within a year's time, a tree has blossomed, born fruit, and from this has come a highly treasured oil . . . natural in every sense, made only by mechanical processes.

After a civilization of 5,000 years, and notwithstanding discoveries of the 20th Century, mankind has not found a cooking oil more perfect than olive oil: a pure and natural product.

Cooking with Spanish Olive Oil:

Helpful Hints

Easily stored . . . easily used . . . Spanish olive oil can quickly become an integral part of practically any food preparation activity in your kitchen. Olive oil takes on new meaning when you begin to realize its versatility. Long recognized for its role in salad dressings, olive oil can also add moisture to baked foods; it can tenderize cheaper cuts of meat; it can prevent broiled meats from drying out; it can reduce acidity from tomatoes . . . and much more. You can use olive oil when you bake, barbecue, broil, marinate, braise, saute, fry or scramble. And when you use olive oil from Spain for these food preparation methods, you're adding a special flair . . . because Spanish olive oil is exceptionally light and delicate, adding a uniquely elegant flavor. Recipes in this book show how olive oil from Spain can bring new excitement to everything from appetizers to desserts; from soups to salads; from entrees to vegetables. First, though, a few suggestions for general use of Spanish olive oil.

STORE
at room temperature, since olive oil thickens when refrigerated and changes color. Should this happen, let the oil stand at room temperature. It will regain its light, liquid gold color.

BOIL
pasta in water with a small amount of olive oil; prevents noodles from sticking.

BAKE
with olive oil. It gives extra moistness to cakes and cobblers; helps retain freshness.

BRAISE
meat in olive oil; adds flavor during browning. Then cook slowly in small amount of liquid.

BARBECUE
any meat, poultry or fish with olive oil, using it as a basting ingredient. Helps retain moisture.

BROIL
fish, steaks, chops or poultry after first brushing with olive oil; seals in rich moistness.

FRY

any meat, fish or vegetable in olive oil to add flavor and keep from sticking, without danger of food becoming too greasy.

ROAST

poultry or meat that has first been brushed with olive oil, to help seal in natural juices. Baste with more oil at intervals, adding delicate flavor to the meat.

SIMMER

a tablespoon of olive oil with rice as it is cooking; helps keep rice grains separate.

MARINATE

any meat in olive oil before cooking; adds flavor; tenderizes, too. Because Spanish olive oil is so delicate, it allows other herbs and spices to blend better; never overpowers.

SAUTE

foods in a small amount of oil. Don't overcrowd skillet. When you saute onions this way they lose their biting flavor and take on new sweetness; tomatoes lose some of their acidity.

STIR-FRY

vegetables (cut in small pieces) as well as meat for a few minutes in hot olive oil. Cook only until barely tender. Developed by the Chinese, this cooking trick takes on new meaning with Spanish olive oil because of its unique flavor. Stir constantly.

PAN BROIL

in a lightly oiled skillet, uncovered; creates particularly golden brown entrees.

SCRAMBLE

eggs in olive oil, cooking over a low fire, lifting gently as mixture sets. Eggs don't stick and they take on new flavor.

TOSS

vegetables and greens with oil and seasonings FIRST, when making a salad. Then toss again, adding a dash of vinegar. By adding oil first, you provide a natural coating of oil and this prevents greens from wilting.

12

The American Way... with Olive Oil

American cooking reflects the melting
pot concept of its immigrants. Over the years,
family recipes have changed with the
development of this land. Pure Spanish olive oil,
when used with variations of traditional
American dishes, adds new flavor, new taste
appeal. Long popular with foreign fare, olive oil
is equally at home with standard favorites
in all parts of the United States . . .
as you'll discover in this section.

Before the Meal:

Flavor is all-important for appetizers, soups and dips . . . designed to whet the appetite. Spanish olive oil enhances these recipes, suitable as mealtime "openers" or partytime fare.

Garlic Olives

1 jar pimiento-stuffed green olives
1 can pitted black olives
1 cup Spanish olive oil
4 cloves garlic, crushed
2 tablespoons vinegar

Combine ingredients. Cover and refrigerate. Let stand 24 hours before serving.

Special Curry Dip

2 tablespoons Spanish olive oil
2 teaspoons hot curry powder
1 tablespoon diced onions
1 tablespoon chopped parsley
1 teaspoon dried dill weed
1 teaspoon monosodium glutamate (MSG)
1 cup sour cream
1 cup Spanish mayonnaise

In small saucepan, heat olive oil with curry powder. Cook gently over low heat for 3 minutes. Stir in remaining ingredients. Chill at least 3 hours or overnight. Use as dip for raw vegetables, shrimp, chips and crackers. Makes about 2 cups of dip.

```
CALORIES PER TABLESPOON .......................... 72
GRAMS OF PROTEIN PER TABLESPOON ............... 0
GRAMS OF CARBOHYDRATE PER TABLESPOON ........ 0
GRAMS OF FAT PER TABLESPOON ..................... 7
```

Eggplant Caviar

2 medium eggplants
1 cup water
1 cup drained sliced baby tomatoes
1 tablespoon tomato paste
1 clove garlic, crushed
1 teaspoon lemon juice
1 teaspoon vinegar
1/4 cup Spanish olive oil
1 tablespoon capers
   Few drops Tabasco sauce
1 tablespoon minced onion
1 teaspoon sugar

Peel and slice eggplant. Cook in 1 cup water until tender. Drain and mash. Combine with remaining ingredients. Chill several hours or overnight. Serve as spread for bread or crackers. Makes 2 1/3 cups.

```
CALORIES PER TABLESPOON .......................... 18
GRAMS OF PROTEIN PER TABLESPOON ............... 0
GRAMS OF CARBOHYDRATE PER TABLESPOON ........ 1
GRAMS OF FAT PER TABLESPOON ..................... 1
```

Spicy Almonds

Blanch shelled almonds with boiling water; rub off skins, cool, then saute in Spanish olive oil until golden; drain on absorbent papers, sprinkle generously with salt, powdered cumin, powdered ginger or curry powder.

Spanish Meat Balls

    1 pound lean ground pork or beef
    1 or 2 cloves garlic, crushed
    1 tablespoon minced parsley
    1 egg, beaten
  3/4 teaspoon salt
    1 tablespoon Spanish olive oil
  1/2 cup fine bread crumbs
  1/4 cup Spanish olive oil

Combine all ingredients except 1/4 cup of olive oil and knead with fingers until smooth. Form into 1/2-inch balls. Saute in olive oil until well-browned on all sides. Serve hot on toothpicks, or keep warm in a chafing dish if desired, adding just enough sherry to form a sauce to keep meatballs from drying out. Makes about 25 meatballs.

CALORIES PER SERVING 71
GRAMS OF PROTEIN PER SERVING 4
GRAMS OF CARBOHYDRATE PER SERVING 1
GRAMS OF FAT PER SERVING 5

Chicken Bites

    2 whole chicken breasts, split, boned and
       skinned
    1 egg, beaten
    1 teaspoon salt
  1/4 teaspoon pepper
    1 cup seasoned bread crumbs
  1/2 cup Spanish olive oil

Cut chicken into about 35 bite-size pieces. Mix egg, salt, pepper. Dip chicken pieces into egg mixture. Coat with crumbs. Heat olive oil in large skillet, saute chicken until browned on both sides. Serve immediately on wooden picks. Makes 35 appetizers.

CALORIES PER SERVING 52
GRAMS OF PROTEIN PER SERVING 3
GRAMS OF CARBOHYDRATE PER SERVING 1
GRAMS OF FAT PER SERVING 3

Canned Meat Bites

    1 can (12 oz.) luncheon meat or ham
    1 green pepper, cut in squares
  1/2 cup Spanish olive oil
    1 teaspoon curry powder, powdered cumin or
       fennel
  1/8 teaspoon dry mustard
       Salt and pepper

Cut meat into 1/2-inch cubes, marinate meat with green pepper in olive oil, curry and dry mustard. Season to taste with salt and pepper. Skewer meat with green pepper on either side; hold over barbecue fire until sizzling. Makes 45 appetizers.

CALORIES PER SERVING 44
GRAMS OF PROTEIN PER SERVING 1
GRAMS OF CARBOHYDRATE PER SERVING 0
GRAMS OF FAT PER SERVING 4

Fried Sole Appetizer

- 1 pound sole fillets
- 2 eggs, separated
- 1/4 cup flour
- 2 tablespoons water
- 1/4 teaspoon salt
- 1 1/2 cups Spanish olive oil

CAPER SAUCE
- 3/4 cup mayonnaise
- 1/4 cup capers

Cut fish into pieces 1/2-inch wide by 1 1/2-inch long. Beat egg whites until stiff. Then beat egg yolks with flour, water and salt. Fold whites into yolk mixture, stirring until smooth. Heat olive oil in a skillet. Dip fish pieces into batter; fry in hot olive oil until crisp on both sides. Drain on paper towels. Serve hot with caper sauce. If desired these may be prepared early in the day. At serving time, heat oven to 500°F., place fish pieces on baking sheet, place in oven, turn oven immediately down to 200°F. Fish will keep warm and crisp without burning for 20 minutes. Makes 36 pieces.

To make sauce: Combine mayonnaise and capers in a bowl; chill until ready to serve. Sprinkle with parsley. Makes 1 cup.

```
CALORIES PER PIECE ........................... 149
GRAMS OF PROTEIN PER PIECE ................... 4
GRAMS OF CARBOHYDRATE PER PIECE .............. 0
GRAMS OF FAT PER PIECE ....................... 14
```

Chicken Livers en Brochette

- 1 pound chicken livers
- 1/2 cup Spanish olive oil
- 1/2 cup finely chopped onion
- 1 teaspoon paprika
- 1/2 teaspoon salt
- 1/2 teaspoon basil
- 1 teaspoon vinegar
- 1 green pepper cut into 1-inch pieces

Combine all ingredients; marinate at least one hour. Thread onto skewers alternating livers with green peppers. Broil about 10 minutes until livers are cooked, turning once. Serve hot. Makes 6 servings.

```
CALORIES PER SERVING ......................... 277
GRAMS OF PROTEIN PER SERVING ................. 16
GRAMS OF CARBOHYDRATE PER SERVING ............ 3
GRAMS OF FAT PER SERVING ..................... 21
```

Shrimp Toast

- 1/2 pound uncooked shrimp
- 6 water chestnuts, finely chopped
- 1 egg, slightly beaten
- 1 teaspoon salt
- 1 teaspoon Spanish sherry
- 1/2 teaspoon ground ginger
- 1 tablespoon chopped scallion
- 1/2 teaspoon sugar
- 1 tablespoon cornstarch
- 8 slices white bread
- 2 cups Spanish olive oil

Clean and chop shrimp. Mix with water chestnuts, egg, salt, sherry, ginger, scallion, sugar and cornstarch. Trim crusts from bread. Cut each slice into quarters. Spread 1 heaping tablespoon shrimp mixture over each quarter of bread. Heat olive oil to 375°F. in small saucepan. Deep fry with shrimp side down for about 30 seconds. Turn over; fry for 5 seconds until the bread is slightly browned. Drain on absorbent toweling. Serve hot. Makes 32 appetizers.

```
CALORIES PER APPETIZER ....................... 150
GRAMS OF PROTEIN PER APPETIZER ............... 2
GRAMS OF CARBOHYDRATE PER APPETIZER .......... 3
GRAMS OF FAT PER APPETIZER ................... 14
```

Crabmeat Pate

- 1 can (6 oz.) crabmeat
- 1/4 cup shelled, chopped almonds
- 1/4 cup Spanish olive oil
- 2 tablespoons finely minced parsely
- 1/4 teaspoon salt
- 1 tablespoon dry sherry

Clean crabmeat. Saute almonds in 2 tablespoons of the olive oil until browned; drain, cool, then chop fine. Combine crabmeat, nuts, parsely and salt in blender container and blend at low speed; slowly add 2 tablespoons olive oil and dry sherry; blend until smooth. Serve in tiny patty shells, or on toast rounds, or in bowl for guests to make their own canapes. Makes 16 canapes.

```
CALORIES PER CANAPE .......................... 47
GRAMS OF PROTEIN PER CANAPE .................. 2
GRAMS OF CARBOHYDRATE PER CANAPE ............. 0
GRAMS OF FAT PER CANAPE ...................... 4
```

Chicken Salad Canapes

    1 cup diced cooked or canned chicken
    2 pimientos (from can), drained and minced
  1/2 cup cooked peas
       Pinch of powdered cumin
    2 tablespoons mayonnaise
    6 slices of bread
  1/4 cup Spanish olive oil

Place the diced chicken, the pimientos, peas, cumin and mayonnaise in a bowl, toss lightly to blend. Trim off bread crusts and cut each slice into 4 squares; saute until very lightly colored on each side in the olive oil. When ready to serve, place the sauteed bread squares in a hot oven to crisp, then serve topped with a spoonful (about 1 tablespoon each) of the chicken mixture. Makes 24 canapes.

CALORIES PER SERVING 64
GRAMS OF PROTEIN PER SERVING 2
GRAMS OF CARBOHYDRATE PER SERVING 3
GRAMS OF FAT PER SERVING 4

Shrimp with Garlic

1 1/2 pounds (about 35) raw shrimp in the shell
   3/4 cup Spanish olive oil
   1/4 cup lemon juice
     3 cloves garlic, minced
     1 tablespoon chopped parsley
   1/2 teaspoon salt
     2 tablespoons lemon juice

Shell shrimp leaving tails intact; devein. Combine rest of ingredients and marinate shrimp in the mixture for at least an hour. Bake at 450°F. for 5 to 7 minutes or until shrimp are pink. Serve sizzling hot as an appetizer to be speared with wooden picks. Makes 35 appetizers.

CALORIES PER APPETIZER 61
GRAMS OF PROTEIN PER APPETIZER 3
GRAMS OF CARBOHYDRATE PER APPETIZER 0
GRAMS OF FAT PER APPETIZER 4

Make Cheese Pate with Dried-up Cheese

When wedges of cheese become dried out, there is no need to throw them away. Simply grate or shred the cheese, beat into a paste with a tablespoon or two of Spanish olive oil and a tablespoon of brandy or bourbon, and you have an excellent spread for hors d'oeuvres. Use any cheese or combination of cheese. For a softer spread, add a little cream cheese, or even a bit of leftover dessert cheese, such as Camembert or Liederkranz.

Party Omelette

   12 slices bacon
    3 tablespoons Spanish olive oil
    1 cup diced green pepper
  1/2 cup chopped onion
    6 eggs, beaten
    1 cup heavy cream
    1 teaspoon salt
  1/4 teaspoon ground nutmeg
  1/8 teaspoon pepper
  1/4 pound Swiss cheese, diced
    1 can (7 oz.) tuna, drained and flaked

Fry bacon until crisp; drain and crumble. Meanwhile, heat olive oil in medium skillet and saute green pepper and onion until tender, but not browned. Grease the inside of a 9-inch springform pan with additional Spanish olive oil. Place it on a baking sheet and preheat both in 450°F. oven for 4 or 5 minutes. Combine eggs, cream, seasonings, cheese, tuna, bacon, and sauteed onion and green peppers. Pour into preheated pan. Bake uncovered at 450°F. for 10 minutes; then reduce heat to 350°F. and continue baking for 10 more minutes. Remove sides of pan and cut tortilla into 16 wedges. Serve hot or cold. Makes 16 servings.

CALORIES PER SERVING 200
GRAMS OF PROTEIN PER SERVING 9
GRAMS OF CARBOHYDRATE PER SERVING 1
GRAMS OF FAT PER SERVING 17

Avocado Dunk

2 ripe avocados
1/2 cup Spanish mayonnaise
3 tablespoons lemon juice
1 teaspoon chili powder
1 small clove garlic, pressed
1/4 teaspoon Tabasco sauce
1/4 teaspoon salt

Mash avocados with fork or place in blender and blend until smooth. Stir in remaining ingredients. Refrigerate for about 1 hour before serving to let flavors blend. Serve as a dip for raw vegetable such as cauliflower buds, green pepper slices, carrot and cucumber sticks. Makes 1 1/2 cups.

CALORIES PER TABLESPOON 62
GRAMS OF PROTEIN PER TABLESPOON 0
GRAMS OF CARBOHYDRATE PER TABLESPOON 1
GRAMS OF FAT PER TABLESPOON 6

Baby Carrots Vinaigrette

2 cans (15 oz. *each*) baby carrots, drained
1/2 cup Spanish olive oil
1/4 cup red wine vinegar
1/2 teaspoon salt
1/4 teaspoon black pepper
1/4 cup minced parsley
3 slices of onion

Combine ingredients in a bowl; cover and refrigerate 2 hours or more. Remove onions before serving, if desired. Makes 8 servings.

CALORIES PER SERVING 159
GRAMS OF PROTEIN PER SERVING 1
GRAMS OF CARBOHYDRATE PER SERVING 8
GRAMS OF FAT PER SERVING 14

Snappy Cheese Wedges

12 slices white bread
1/2 cup processed Cheddar cheese spread
1 teaspoon Spanish olive oil
1/4 teaspoon Tabasco sauce
1/4 teaspoon prepared mustard
Rolled anchovies (optional)

Remove crusts from bread. Slice diagonally to make 4 wedges from each slice. Blend cheese spread, olive oil, Tabasco and mustard. Spread on bread wedges. Place in 400°F. oven for 5 minutes or until cheese is bubbly. Place rolled anchovies on wedges, if desired. Serve immediately. Makes 48.

CALORIES PER WEDGE 24
GRAMS OF PROTEIN PER WEDGE 0
GRAMS OF CARBOHYDRATE PER WEDGE 3
GRAMS OF FAT PER WEDGE 0

Beef Strips Sesame

4 pounds boneless rolled beef rump roast
4 cups cocktail vegetable juice
1/2 cup Spanish olive oil
1/2 cup sherry
1/2 cup soy sauce
1/2 cup toasted sesame seed
2 tablespoons sugar
1 large clove garlic, minced
1 cup diced pimiento
1/2 cup thinly sliced onion
Salad greens
Green pepper rings

In roasting pan, roast meat fat-side up at 325°F. for about 1 1/2 hours. (Rare — 25 minutes per lb. or 140°F. on meat thermometer.) Cool; trim fat. Slice meat into thin strips (3" x 1/2"). Meanwhile, in shallow baking dish, combine vegetable juice, olive oil, sherry, soy sauce, sesame seed, sugar and garlic. Add meat; refrigerate overnight. Stir in pimiento and onion. Drain meat mixture, reserving marinade; arrange on salad greens. Garnish with green pepper. Serve with marinade. Makes 12 servings.

CALORIES PER SERVING 255
GRAMS OF PROTEIN PER SERVING 18
GRAMS OF CARBOHYDRATE PER SERVING 8
GRAMS OF FAT PER SERVING 15

Yogurt Soup

3 cans (10 3/4 oz. *each*) condensed cream of chicken soup
1 1/2 cups plain yogurt
1/4 cup honey
1/2 teaspoon ground mace
3 soup cans milk

In saucepan, blend soup, yogurt, honey, and mace. Stir in milk. Heat, stirring occasionally. Garnish with watercress, if desired. Makes 12 servings.

CALORIES PER SERVING 152
GRAMS OF PROTEIN PER SERVING 5
GRAMS OF CARBOHYDRATE PER SERVING 16
GRAMS OF FAT PER SERVING 7

Pasta Pot

1/2 cup chopped green pepper
1 large clove garlic, minced
1/4 teaspoon rosemary leaves, crushed
2 tablespoons Spanish olive oil
3 cans (10³/4 oz. *each*) condensed tomato
   soup
3 soup cans water
1 can (16 oz.) chick peas or kidney beans,
   drained
1 cup cooked small shell macaroni or elbow
   macaroni
2 teaspoons chopped anchovy

In large saucepan, saute pepper with garlic and rosemary in olive oil until tender. Stir in soup and water. Add remaining ingredients. Heat; stir occasionally. Makes 10 servings.

```
CALORIES PER SERVING ........................... 162
GRAMS OF PROTEIN PER SERVING ................. 5
GRAMS OF CARBOHYDRATE PER SERVING ........... 24
GRAMS OF FAT PER SERVING ....................... 5
```

Antipasto Loaves

1 medium head bibb lettuce, shredded
   (4 cups)
1/4 cup chopped ripe olives
1/4 cup Spanish olive oil
1 tablespoon vinegar
1/4 teaspoon salt
   Dash *each* pepper, oregano, basil and
   garlic salt
2 loaves (1 lb. *each*) Italian bread, slit
1/2 pound thinly sliced roast beef
1/4 pound sliced fresh mushrooms
1/2 pound thinly sliced salami
4 hard-cooked eggs, sliced
   Oregano leaves

Combine lettuce, olives, olive oil, vinegar, salt and seasonings. On each loaf of bread, place single layer of beef, mushrooms, salami, eggs, and lettuce mixture. Sprinkle with oregano. Cut each sandwich into 4 servings. Makes 8 sandwiches.

```
CALORIES PER SERVING ........................... 581
GRAMS OF PROTEIN PER SERVING ................. 24
GRAMS OF CARBOHYDRATE PER SERVING ........... 65
GRAMS OF FAT PER SERVING ...................... 22
```

Lentil Soup

1 cup chopped onion
1 cup diced green pepper
1/4 cup diced pimiento
1/4 cup Spanish olive oil
2 tablespoons flour
1 can (16. oz.) tomatoes with liquid
2 cups sliced carrots
1 cup sliced celery
1 tablespoon salt
1 pound dry lentils
8 cups water

In 6-quart pressure cooker, saute onion, green pepper and pimiento in olive oil until very soft. Stir in flour, cook until bubbling but do not brown. Add tomatoes, carrots, celery, salt, lentils and water. Close cover securely. Place pressure regulator on vent pipe. Cook for 15 minutes. Let pressure reduce of its own accord — about 25 minutes. (To cook in Dutch oven, simmer, covered, for 2 hours.) Serve with a tossed salad and hot rolls. Makes 10 servings.

```
CALORIES PER SERVING ........................... 245
GRAMS OF PROTEIN PER SERVING ................. 12
GRAMS OF CARBOHYDRATE PER SERVING ........... 36
GRAMS OF FAT PER SERVING ....................... 6
```

Spanish Potato Soup

2 medium onions, chopped fine
1/4 cup Spanish olive oil
1 1/2 quarts chicken or beef stock
1/4 cup dry sherry or dry white wine
6 potatoes, peeled, diced
   Salt to taste

Saute onions in olive oil until golden. Add chicken or beef stock and wine; bring to a boil and add the potatoes. Cook 20 to 30 minutes until tender. Lift potatoes from broth; mash or beat with mixer until smooth. Return to broth. Makes 8 servings.

```
CALORIES PER SERVING ........................... 167
GRAMS OF PROTEIN PER SERVING ................. 6
GRAMS OF CARBOHYDRATE PER SERVING ........... 18
GRAMS OF FAT PER SERVING ....................... 7
```

Spanish Almond Soup

  3 **cans (10¹/₂ oz. *each*) condensed consomme**
2¹/₂ **soup cans water**
 ¹/₂ **cup ground almonds**
 ¹/₄ **cup Spanish olive oil**
  6 **slices toast, crusts trimmed**
 ¹/₃ **cup grated Parmesan cheese**
 ¹/₂ **cup toasted sliced almonds**

In a large saucepan, combine consomme and water. Heat, stirring occasionally. In bowl, combine ground almonds and olive oil; stir into soup. Meanwhile, sprinkle toast with cheese; broil until cheese is golden. Garnish soup with toast and sliced almonds. Makes 8 servings.

CALORIES PER SERVING 342
GRAMS OF PROTEIN PER SERVING 11
GRAMS OF CARBOHYDRATE PER SERVING 16
GRAMS OF FAT PER SERVING 28

Royal Soup

  1 **chicken breast, chopped**
¹/₄ **pound lean ham, chopped**
  1 **tablespoon butter**
  1 **tablespoon Spanish olive oil**
  3 **slices of onion, minced**
  4 **chicken bouillon cubes or envelopes of chicken stock concentrate**
  6 **cups water**
¹/₄ **cup medium sweet sherry**
  6 **hard-cooked eggs, chopped**
    Croutons, sauteed until crisp in Spanish olive oil

Place chopped chicken and ham in a pan with butter and olive oil. Cook over moderate heat 5 minutes. Add onion; cook until golden. Add bouillon cubes, water and sherry. Simmer uncovered 15-20 minutes. Add eggs, simmer 2-3 minutes. Top with croutons before serving. Makes 8 servings.

CALORIES PER SERVING 151
GRAMS OF PROTEIN PER SERVING 13
GRAMS OF CARBOHYDRATE PER SERVING 1
GRAMS OF FAT PER SERVING 8

Quarter-Hour Soup

  1 **package (8 oz.) frozen chicken livers, thawed and chopped**
¹/₂ **pound raw shrimp, shelled, deveined, and chopped**
  1 **clove garlic, minced**
¹/₈ **teaspoon saffron**
³/₄ **cup Spanish olive oil**
  1 **can (10¹/₂ oz.) condensed onion soup**
  1 **can (11 oz.) condensed bisque of tomato soup**
  2 **soup cans water**
  1 **hard-cooked egg, chopped**
¹/₂ **cup cooked rice**
  1 **tablespoon chopped parsley**
  4 **slices bread, cut in cubes**

In large saucepan, saute livers, shrimp, garlic and saffron in ¹/₄ cup olive oil for about 3 minutes, or until done. Add soups, water, egg, rice, and parsley. Heat, stirring occasionally. Heat remaining olive oil in a skillet and saute bread cubes gently until crisp; drain and use to garnish soup. Makes 6 servings.

CALORIES PER SERVING 464
GRAMS OF PROTEIN PER SERVING 21
GRAMS OF CARBOHYDRATE PER SERVING 19
GRAMS OF FAT PER SERVING 33

Main Dishes:

Any Meat, Seafood or Poultry entree benefits from the use of olive oil in its preparation . . . whether for sauteeing, marinating or in sauces. Even the most everyday type of dish takes on special flavor when Spanish olive oil is used.

MEAT

Veal Chops Caprice

  4 thick loin veal chops
  1 tablespoon flour
1/2 teaspoon onion salt
1/2 teaspoon paprika
  2 tablespoons Spanish olive oil
  4 slices Swiss Emmanthaler cheese

Rub both sides of chops with mixture of flour, onion salt and paprika. Heat olive oil in heavy skillet; brown the chops over moderate heat until golden on each side; cover, cook over low heat 10 minutes longer. Place chops in heat-proof shallow casserole, top each chop with a slice of cheese, set aside until ready for dinner. About 8 minutes before serving, place 4 inches from heat in broiler, heat until cheese is melted and bubbly, faintly tinged with gold. Makes 4 servings.

CALORIES PER SERVING 635
GRAMS OF PROTEIN PER SERVING 31
GRAMS OF CARBOHYDRATE PER SERVING 1
GRAMS OF FAT PER SERVING 54

Grilled Dill Steak

3/4 cup Spanish olive oil
3/4 cup dill pickle liquid
1/3 cup sliced dill pickles
  1 clove garlic, minced
  3 pounds beef top round (about 1 1/2 to 2-in. thick)
    Salt and pepper

Combine olive oil, pickle liquid, sliced pickles and garlic in large shallow dish. Add meat and turn until coated. Cover and marinate overnight, turning meat once. Remove meat to grill or broiler rack, reserving marinade. Cook 6 inches from source of heat for about 14 to 17 minutes per side for medium doneness. Brush meat with additional marinade during grilling and sprinkle each side with salt and pepper after grilling. (If cooked in a broiler, catch pan juices and pour over meat before serving.) Cut meat diagonally across grain into thin slices. Makes 8 servings.

CALORIES PER SERVING 381
GRAMS OF PROTEIN PER SERVING 32
GRAMS OF CARBOHYDRATE PER SERVING 1
GRAMS OF FAT PER SERVING 25

Rosemary Lamb Shanks Valencia

      6 lamb shanks
  1/4 cup flour
      1 teaspoon salt
  1/2 teaspoon pepper
      1 teaspoon paprika
  1/4 cup Spanish olive oil
      1 teaspoon rosemary, crushed
      1 cup water
  1/2 teaspoon salt
      3 orange slices, cut in half

Coat lamb shanks with mixture of flour, salt, pepper and paprika. Place in shallow pan or baking dish. Pour olive oil over all. Sprinkle with rosemary. Bake uncovered at 350°F. for 2 1/2 to 3 hours, turning occasionally, until crisp on the outside.
To make gravy, take 1 tablespoon of the drippings from the meat and blend in 1 tablespoon flour (or 1 tablespoon of remaining flour mixture used to coat meat). Stir in 1 cup water and 1/2 teaspoon salt. Cook and stir over medium heat until thickened. Garnish with orange slices. Spoon gravy over all. Makes 6 servings.

```
CALORIES PER SERVING ............................. 159
GRAMS OF PROTEIN PER SERVING ................... 8
GRAMS OF CARBOHYDRATE PER SERVING ............ 4
GRAMS OF FAT PER SERVING ........................ 11
```

Beef Stuffed Onions

      3 sweet Spanish onions
      1 pound ground beef
  1/3 cup chopped celery
      1 can (6 oz.) tomato sauce
      1 teaspoon salt
  1/4 teaspoon dry mustard
  1/2 teaspoon chili powder
  1/4 cup dry bread crumbs
      1 tablespoon Spanish olive oil

Peel and halve onions. Place cut side up in boiling salted water; cover and simmer for 20 minutes. Remove center portions of onion halves and chop enough to make 1/3 cup. (Store remaining center portions of onion in plastic bag and refrigerate to use later in recipes calling for chopped onions.)

Brown ground beef in skillet. Add celery and chopped onion and cook until tender. Stir in tomato sauce, salt, dry mustard and chili powder. Stuff onion halves with beef mixture and sprinkle with bread crumbs browned in olive oil. Bake for 30 minutes at 350°F. Makes 6 servings.

```
CALORIES PER SERVING ............................. 244
GRAMS OF PROTEIN PER SERVING ................... 16
GRAMS OF CARBOHYDRATE PER SERVING ............ 10
GRAMS OF FAT PER SERVING ........................ 15
```

Lamb Cakes with Garlic Sauce

      2 pounds ground lamb
    12 pitted black olives, minced
      1 onion, minced
  1/4 cup Spanish olive oil
  1/3 cup bread crumbs
      1 tablespoon water
      1 egg
  1/2 teaspoon allspice
      Salt and pepper
      4 slices bread, toasted
      Garlic Sauce

Combine lamb and olives. Saute onion in 1 tablespoon of the oil; stir into lamb mixture. Stir in bread crumbs, water, egg, allspice, salt and pepper. Form into 8 patties; saute in remaining oil until browned and meat is cooked through. Cut each slice of bread in half, top with a lamb pattie, and serve with Garlic Sauce. Makes 8 servings.

Garlic Sauce

      1 medium potato, peeled and cubed
      2 cloves garlic, minced
      1 cup Spanish olive oil
      2 tablespoons red wine vinegar
      Salt and pepper

Cook potato in small saucepan in enough water to cover. Drain and mash. Stir in garlic. Gradually beat in olive oil. Stir in vinegar and salt and pepper.

```
CALORIES PER SERVING ............................. 503
GRAMS OF PROTEIN PER SERVING ................... 16
GRAMS OF CARBOHYDRATE PER SERVING ............ 12
GRAMS OF FAT PER SERVING ........................ 43
```

Mandarin Spareribs

4 pounds pork spareribs
  Water
2 tablespoons salt
1 teaspoon freshly ground black pepper
2 pieces (about 2 inches long *each*) fresh
    ginger root, peeled and cut into thin slices
1 cup sugar
1 cup catsup
1 cup soy sauce
1/4 cup Spanish olive oil

Cut spareribs into 5- or 6-rib sections. Place in large saucepan or Dutch Oven. Cover with water, add salt, pepper and ginger. Bring to a boil, cover, reduce heat, and simmer for 1 hour. Meanwhile, combine sugar, catsup, soy sauce, and olive oil. Drain ribs and immediately cover with catsup mixture. Cover and refrigerate overnight. Place ribs on baking sheet and bake at 325°F. for 1 1/2 hours, basting frequently with remaining marinade. Cut into 1-rib sections to serve. Makes 4 servings.

CALORIES PER SERVING 1068
GRAMS OF PROTEIN PER SERVING 36
GRAMS OF CARBOHYDRATE PER SERVING 24
GRAMS OF FAT PER SERVING 91

Spanish Gypsy Lamb Stew

3 pounds boneless lamb from shoulder, cut
    into 1-inch cubes
2 tablespoons Spanish olive oil
1 1/2 teaspoons paprika
2 cloves garlic, crushed
1/8 teaspoon saffron
1 tablespoon flour
1 cup water
1 tablespoon wine vinegar
1 1/2 teaspoons salt

Brown lamb cubes in olive oil; stir in paprika, garlic and saffron. Slowly add flour; when bubbling, add water, wine vinegar and salt. Simmer until meat is very tender when pricked with fork (about 2 hours). Makes 6 servings.

CALORIES PER SERVING 307
GRAMS OF PROTEIN PER SERVING 25
GRAMS OF CARBOHYDRATE PER SERVING 1
GRAMS OF FAT PER SERVING 21

Creamy Chipped Beef and Rice

1 jar (5 oz.) chipped beef
  Boiling water
2 cups water
2 tablespoons Spanish olive oil
1 package (7 oz.) beef-flavored rice mix
1 cup light cream
2 or 3 hard-cooked eggs, cut in slices or
    wedges

Separate slices of beef; cover with boiling water and drain immediately. Cut into 1-inch slices; set aside. Bring 2 cups water, olive oil, and contents of seasoning packet to a full boil in medium saucepan. Add rice mixture; stir well. Cover; remove from heat. Let stand 7 minutes. Stir in beef and cream. Heat over low heat, stirring occasionally. Serve garnished with egg slices. Makes 5 servings.

CALORIES PER SERVING 332
GRAMS OF PROTEIN PER SERVING 9
GRAMS OF CARBOHYDRATE PER SERVING 25
GRAMS OF FAT PER SERVING 20

Barbecued Spareribs

4 pounds pork spareribs
3 cans (8 oz. *each*) tomato sauce
1/3 cup dark brown sugar
3 tablespoons chopped onion
1 clove garlic, crushed
  Juice of 2 lemons
1/3 cup Spanish olive oil
1/2 teaspoon ground white pepper
2 tablespoons aromatic bitters

Have butcher crack spareribs so they can be cut easily after cooking. Wash spareribs and pat dry. Trim excess fat. Combine remaining ingredients and simmer in a saucepan for 10 minutes. Brush spareribs with the sauce and place ribs 8-10 inches above gray coals. Broil, turning frequently and brushing every few minutes with sauce, for 1 hour or until ribs are brown and done. Makes 4 servings.

CALORIES PER SERVING 949
GRAMS OF PROTEIN PER SERVING 23
GRAMS OF CARBOHYDRATE PER SERVING 38
GRAMS OF FAT PER SERVING 78

California Beef Kiev

- 2 pounds beef top or bottom round, sliced 1/2 inch thick
- 1 tablespoon bottled steak sauce
- 1/4 cup chilled butter
- 1 egg
- 1 (2 3/8 oz.) package seasoned coating mix
  Spanish olive oil

Pound beef with mallet. Cut into 6 rectangular pieces. Spread each with 1/2 teaspoon steak sauce. Cut butter into 6 chunks and place one on each piece of beef. Fold two opposite sides of beef over butter, then roll up. Fasten with picks. Dip rolls in egg lightly beaten with fork, then in coating mix. Heat one inch of olive oil in skillet; fry beef rolls, a few at a time over medium high heat, for 3 to 5 minutes until browned. Remove picks. Makes 6 servings.

CALORIES PER SERVING 615
GRAMS OF PROTEIN PER SERVING 52
GRAMS OF CARBOHYDRATE PER SERVING 11
GRAMS OF FAT PER SERVING 38

Pounded Round Steak

- 6 thin slices round steak, 1/2 inch thick
- 2 tablespoons aromatic bitters
- 1/3 cup flour
- 1 1/2 teaspoons salt
- 1/2 teaspoon pepper
- 1/4 cup Spanish olive oil
- 1/4 cup butter or margarine
- 1/2 cup red wine
- 1/2 cup condensed beef broth
- 1 onion, sliced
- 2 teaspoons cornstarch
- 2 tablespoons water

Remove excess fat from meat. Brush meat with bitters on both sides. Mix flour, salt and pepper; sprinkle over meat and pound into steak until well coated. Heat olive oil and butter until sizzling hot; fry steaks quickly about 5 minutes on each side. Place steaks on a platter and keep warm. Add wine, broth and onions to pan drippings and simmer, stirring to loosen all particles. Mix cornstarch and water and stir into gravy.

28

Stir until thickened and then spoon over steaks. Serve with French fried onion rings, if desired. Makes 6 servings.

CALORIES PER SERVING 455
GRAMS OF PROTEIN PER SERVING 44
GRAMS OF CARBOHYDRATE PER SERVING 8
GRAMS OF FAT PER SERVING 22

Barbecued Lamb Steaks

    6 lamb steaks, about 1-inch thick
 1/2 cup Spanish olive oil
 1/4 cup red wine vinegar
    1 tablespoon grated onion
 1/4 teaspoon oregano
 1/2 teaspoon freshly ground black pepper
      Salt

Make slashes about one inch apart in fat around steaks to prevent curling. Make marinade of olive oil, vinegar, onion, oregano and pepper. Pour over steaks and let stand several hours or overnight in refrigerator. Bring to room temperature and drain, reserving marinade. Grill steaks over hot coals about 25 minutes, or to desired degree of doneness, turning and basting several times with the marinade. When done, salt to taste. Makes 6 servings.

CALORIES PER SERVING 286
GRAMS OF PROTEIN PER SERVING 10
GRAMS OF CARBOHYDRATE PER SERVING 0
GRAMS OF FAT PER SERVING 26

Balearic Veal Stew

    2 pounds boneless veal for stew, cut in cubes
 1/4 teaspoon cumin
 1/8 teaspoon cayenne pepper
    2 teaspoons salt
    2 tablespoons flour
 1/4 cup Spanish olive oil
    1 cup minced onion
    2 garlic cloves, minced
    2 tomatoes, peeled and chopped
    4 to 6 potatoes, peeled and quartered
    4 large carrots, scraped and cubed
    1 cup white wine
    1 cup water
    1 tablespoon minced parsley
    1 hard-cooked egg, sliced or cut in eighths

Roll veal in mixture of seasonings and flour. Saute until golden in olive oil. Add onion, garlic and tomatoes; cook until vegetables are very soft. Add potatoes and carrots, cook until golden, adding more olive oil if necessary. Add wine and water, bring to a boil, cover and simmer about 45 minutes or until meat and vegetables are tender. Serve in casserole topped with parsley and egg as garnish. Makes 6 servings.

CALORIES PER SERVING 474
GRAMS OF PROTEIN PER SERVING 28
GRAMS OF CARBOHYDRATE PER SERVING 25
GRAMS OF FAT PER SERVING 25

Liver and Bacon Ragout

- 1 sweet Spanish onion
- 1 pound beef liver
- 1/4 cup flour
- Salt and pepper
- 1/4 cup Spanish olive oil
- 3 potatoes
- 3/4 cup beef broth
- 1/4 teaspoon majoram
- 1 tablespoon chopped parsley

Peel and slice onion. Remove membrane from liver, snip out veins and cut into 4 serving portions. Dredge with flour. Sprinkle with salt and pepper. Brown in 2 tablespoons olive oil. Remove and set aside. Add remaining olive oil to skillet. Saute onion until transparent. Peel and dice potatoes. Add to skillet and saute until lightly browned. Add beef broth, marjoram and liver. Cover and simmer 10 minutes. Sprinkle with parsley. Makes 4 servings

```
CALORIES PER SERVING ............................ 386
GRAMS OF PROTEIN PER SERVING .................... 27
GRAMS OF CARBOHYDRATE PER SERVING ........... 28
GRAMS OF FAT PER SERVING ........................ 17
```

Spanish Rice with Beef

- 1/4 cup Spanish olive oil
- 1 package (8 oz.) beef flavor rice mix
- 1 pound ground beef
- 1 can (6 oz.) sliced mushrooms, drained
- 1/2 cup sliced stuffed olives
- 2 cans (16 oz. each) stewed tomatoes
- 1 cup water
- 1 1/2 tablespoons aromatic bitters
- Salt and pepper
- Additional olives

Heat olive oil and add rice from mix. Cook while stirring until golden brown. Pour mixture into a 2-quart casserole. Sprinkle seasoning mix from package over rice. Cook beef in skillet until brown and crumbly. Drain excess fat and put beef into casserole. Add mushrooms, olives, tomatoes, water and bitters. Stir to blend. Cover and bake in oven at 350°F., for 40 to 45 minutes or until rice is tender. Uncover and fluff mixture with a fork. Season to taste with salt and pepper. Garnish top with additional olive slices. Makes 6 servings.

```
CALORIES PER SERVING ............................ 454
GRAMS OF PROTEIN PER SERVING .................... 19
GRAMS OF CARBOHYDRATE PER SERVING ........... 45
GRAMS OF FAT PER SERVING ........................ 21
```

Wheat Germ Rice with Stir Fry Beef

- 2 cups uncooked rice
- 1/2 cup toasted wheat germ
- 1 1/2 pounds lean boneless beef chuck steak
- Instant unseasoned meat tenderizer
- Pepper
- 1 clove garlic, minced
- 2 tablespoons Spanish olive oil
- 1 package (10 oz.) frozen cut green beans
- 1/2 pound fresh mushrooms, halved or quartered
- 1 can (16 oz.) whole peeled tomatoes, cut in wedges
- 1/2 cup dry sherry or consomme
- 2 tablespoons cornstarch
- 1 1/2 teaspoons salt
- 1 teaspoon basil
- 1 teaspoon tarragon

Cook rice according to directions on package. Mix with wheat germ and pack into greased 6-cup ring mold. Meanwhile tenderize beef according to directions of meat tenderizer. Sprinkle with pepper. Cut beef into thin strips. Cook with garlic in olive oil in large skillet over high heat, tossing and stirring until browned. Add green beans and mushrooms. Cover and continue cooking, stirring often, 5 to 10 minutes or until tender. Add undrained tomato wedges. Stir in wine mixed with cornstarch, salt, basil and tarragon. Cook, stirring until sauce comes to boil and thickens. Invert wheat germ ring onto plate. Fill with stir fry beef. Makes 6 servings.

```
CALORIES PER SERVING ............................ 792
GRAMS OF PROTEIN PER SERVING .................... 35
GRAMS OF CARBOHYDRATE PER SERVING ........... 52
GRAMS OF FAT PER SERVING ........................ 47
```

Wheat Germ is the most nutritious part of the wheat. It's the "heart of the wheat kernel" that germinates when the kernel is planted. Thus the name Wheat Germ.

Old-Fashioned Beef Stew

    1 pound lean beef cubes
    1 tablespoon flour
    2 tablespoons Spanish olive oil
    4 cups tomato juice
1/2 cup diced celery
    6 whole allspice
    1 bay leaf
1/2 teaspoon salt
1/8 teaspoon pepper
    3 potatoes, peeled and cubed
    4 carrots, peeled and sliced
    1 pound small white onions, peeled
    2 cups peas

Coat beef with flour. Heat olive oil in Dutch oven or large saucepan; add meat and brown well. Add 2 cups of the tomato juice, the celery and seasonings. Bring to a boil, cover, reduce heat and simmer 1 1/2 hours. Add remaining tomato juice, potatoes, carrots and onions. Cook, covered, 45 minutes. Add peas; cook 20 minutes or until meat and vegetables are tender. Makes 6 servings.

Beef Stew with Fluffy Dumplings

About 20 minutes before stew is done, spoon Dumpling Batter on top of ingredients. Cook uncovered for 10 minutes; then cover and cook 10 minutes.

Dumpling Batter

1 1/2 cups flour
    2 teaspoons baking powder
3/4 teaspoon salt
    1 egg
3/4 cup milk
    3 tablespoons Spanish olive oil

Mix flour, baking powder and salt. Beat egg with milk and olive oil. Add to flour mixture and stir until just blended.

Dilly Dumplings: Stir 2 teaspoons dried dill weed into batter.

Green Dumplings: Add 1/4 cup chopped fresh parsley to batter.

Spicy Dumplings: Add 1/4 teaspoon ground ginger and a dash of garlic powder and soy sauce to batter.

Speckled Dumplings: Stir 1 teaspoon poppy seeds into batter.

```
CALORIES PER SERVING .............................. 599
GRAMS OF PROTEIN PER SERVING .................... 36
GRAMS OF CARBOHYDRATE PER SERVING ........... 58
GRAMS OF FAT PER SERVING ........................ 24
```

Barbecued Pork Tenderloin

    2 pounds pork tenderloin, cut in 1-inch cubes
1 1/2 teaspoons salt
1/4 teaspoon pepper
    2 zucchini squash (each about 6-in.), thickly
        sliced
1/4 cup Spanish olive oil
    1 red onion, sliced in wedges
       Cherry tomatoes
    1 tablespoon tomato catsup
    1 tablespoon soy sauce
1/2 cup dry red or white wine or dry sherry
1/2 teaspoon dry mustard
1/4 teaspoon oregano

Rub cubes of meat with salt and pepper. Marinate the squash in the olive oil several hours in advance. Arrange on barbecue skewers alternately with slices of onion, cherry tomatoes and the pork. Cook 3 to 4 inches from heat over moderate charcoal fire. After meat starts to brown, brush occasionally with sauce made of olive oil, catsup, soy sauce, wine mustard and oregano. Cook until meat is very brown, about 25 minutes. Makes 6 servings.

```
CALORIES PER SERVING .............................. 477
GRAMS OF PROTEIN PER SERVING .................... 46
GRAMS OF CARBOHYDRATE PER SERVING ...........  5
GRAMS OF FAT PER SERVING ........................ 27
```

SEAFOOD

Fish Fold-Overs

    8 large flounder fillets
    1 teaspoon salt
    2 lemons
    1 package (8 oz.) bread stuffing
    2 tablespoons chopped fresh dill
    1 package (6 oz.) Swiss cheese, finely diced
    1 cup chicken broth
 1/2 cup melted butter
 1/2 cup Spanish olive oil
 1/2 cup cornflake crumbs
    1 tablespoon chopped fresh dill

Sprinkle flounder fillets with salt and lemon juice. In a bowl mix bread stuffing, 2 tablespoons dill, the cheese, and chicken broth. Mix butter and olive oil; add half to stuffing mixture. Spoon stuffing on half of each flounder fillet. Fold uncovered half over stuffing. Place in shallow baking pan which has been brushed with some of the remaining butter/olive oil mixture. Spoon remaining olive oil mixture over stuffed fillets. Sprinkle with cornflake crumbs and dill. Bake at 350°F. for 30 minutes or until fish turns white and flakes easily. Makes 8 servings.

```
CALORIES PER SERVING ............................. 545
GRAMS OF PROTEIN PER SERVING ................... 39
GRAMS OF CARBOHYDRATE PER SERVING .......... 21
GRAMS OF FAT PER SERVING ........................ 33
```

Baked Halibut with Mushroom Sauce

    2 tablespoons Spanish olive oil
 1/2 cup minced fresh mushrooms
    1 carrot, grated
    2 tablespoons minced onion
    1 teaspoon salt
    2 pounds halibut steaks
    1 cup white wine or vegetable bouillon

Brush bottom of shallow casserole with a little of the olive oil. Place the mushrooms,

carrot and onion in the casserole. Sprinkle 1/4 teaspoon salt over the vegetables. Lay fish steaks over vegetables and sprinkle with remaining salt. Brush with remaining olive oil. Bake at 350°F. for 10 minutes; add wine to dish, bake another 30 to 40 minutes until fish flakes easily. Remove fish to serving platter. Spoon vegetables and sauce into saucepan, bring to a boil and cook until sauce is somewhat reduced; spoon sauce over top of fish. Serve with lemon wedges on the side, if desired. Makes 6 servings.

```
CALORIES PER SERVING ............................. 324
GRAMS OF PROTEIN PER SERVING ................... 25
GRAMS OF CARBOYDRATE PER SERVING ............. 36
GRAMS OF FAT PER SERVING ........................ 6
```

Halibut Parmigiana

    2 pounds halibut steaks
    2 eggs, beaten
 1/2 teaspoon salt
 1/4 teaspoon pepper
 3/4 cup fine dry bread crumbs
 1/3 cup grated Parmesan cheese
 1/3 cup Spanish olive oil
    1 can (8 oz.) tomato sauce
    2 tablespoons dry red wine
 1/4 cup sliced olives
 1/4 teaspoon basil
 1/4 teaspoon salt
    1 clove garlic, crushed
      Dash pepper
    6 slices Mozzarella cheese

If halibut is frozen, defrost in refrigerator. Beat eggs with 1/2 teaspoon salt and 1/4 teaspoon pepper. Combine bread crumbs and grated Parmesan cheese. Dip halibut steaks in egg mixture, drain slightly, then dip in crumb mixture. Heat olive oil in skillet and fry halibut steaks until browned on each side. Remove to shallow baking dish. Combine remaining ingredients except Mozzarella cheese. Spoon over halibut. Place slice of Mozzarella cheese on top. Place under broiler until cheese is melted and bubbly. Makes 6 servings.

```
CALORIES PER SERVING ............................. 572
GRAMS OF PROTEIN PER SERVING ................... 48
GRAMS OF CARBOHYDRATE PER SERVING ............ 13
GRAMS OF FAT PER SERVING ........................ 34
```

Pickled Fish

1½ pounds halibut, striped bass or other fish,
  cut in ¾-inch thick steaks
1 teaspoon monosodium glutamate
¾ teaspoon salt
¼ teaspoon pepper
¼ cup Spanish olive oil
½ cup onion rings
½ cup sliced pimiento-stuffed olives
2 teaspoons dry mint flakes or 1 tablespoon
  chopped fresh mint
½ cup vinegar
  Salad greens

Sprinkle fish with monosodium glutamate, salt and pepper. Lightly brown fish in heated olive oil in skillet; transfer to shallow casserole. In same skillet, cook onion until soft and yellow about 3 minutes; add olives, mint flakes and vinegar; pour over fish. Cover and refrigerate 6 to 8 hours or overnight. Drain and serve on salad greens. Makes 6 servings.

```
CALORIES PER SERVING .............................. 211
GRAMS OF PROTEIN PER SERVING .................... 23
GRAMS OF CARBOHYDRATE PER SERVING ............ 2
GRAMS OF FAT PER SERVING ........................ 11
```

Shrimp Vinaigrette

1½ pounds medium shrimp in the shell
¼ cup vinegar
2 tablespoons Spanish olive oil
½ teaspoon salt
  Dash of Tabasco sauce, or cayenne pepper
2 hard-cooked egg yolks, minced
1 tablespoon minced parsley
2 tablespoons finely minced green pepper
2 tablespoons capers
1 tablespoon grated onion

Cook and shell fresh shrimp. Combine all other ingredients; add shrimp and refrigerate for at least 6 hours. Serve cold. Makes 6 servings.

```
CALORIES PER SERVING .............................. 167
GRAMS OF PROTEIN PER SERVING .................... 22
GRAMS OF CARBOHYDRATE PER SERVING ............ 2
GRAMS OF FAT PER SERVING ........................ 7
```

Marinated Shrimp with Olives and Mushrooms

1 pound fresh mushrooms, quartered
1 cup water
⅓ cup Spanish olive oil
⅔ cup vinegar
2 tablespoons lemon juice
2 cloves garlic, halved
1¼ teaspoons salt
½ teaspoon thyme leaves
½ teaspoon peppercorns
⅛ teaspoon nutmeg
2 bay leaves
¾ cup pimiento-stuffed olives
2 pounds medium shrimp, cleaned and
  cooked

Combine mushrooms, water, olive oil, vinegar, lemon juice, garlic and seasonings in saucepan. Bring to a boil, cover, and cook for 5 minutes. Pour into a bowl; add olives and shrimp and cool. Cover and refrigerate 6 to 8 hours or overnight before serving. Makes 8 servings.

```
CALORIES PER SERVING .............................. 210
GRAMS OF PROTEIN PER SERVING .................... 22
GRAMS OF CARBOHYDRATE PER SERVING ............ 4
GRAMS OF FAT PER SERVING ........................ 11
```

Salsa

2 tablespoons finely chopped onion
¼ cup Spanish olive oil
¼ cup flour
1 teaspoon salt
2 cups water
1 cup sour cream
2 teaspoons prepared horseradish
2 avocados, diced

Saute onion in olive oil until barely tender. Blend in flour and salt. Gradually add water, stirring until smooth. Cook and stir over medium heat until thickened. Remove from heat and stir in sour cream, horseradish and diced avocado. Serve as sauce for fish and seafood. Makes 6 servings.

```
CALORIES PER SERVING .............................. 46
GRAMS OF PROTEIN PER SERVING .................... 1
GRAMS OF CARBOHYDRATE PER SERVING ............ 6
GRAMS OF FAT PER SERVING ........................ 2
```

Rolled Olive Stuffed Flounder

    2 tablespoons Spanish olive oil
    2 tablespoons grated onion
 1/2 cup grated carrot
 1/2 cup chopped pimiento-stuffed olives
    1 tablespoon dry bread crumbs
    1 tablespoon chopped parsley
    2 pounds fresh or frozen fillet of flounder
    2 tablespoons water
    3 tablespoons dry sherry
 1/4 cup lemon juice
 1/2 teaspoon seasoned salt
    2 tablespoons butter or margarine
      Sliced pimiento-stuffed olives

Heat olive oil; add onion, carrot and 1/2 cup chopped olives. Cook over low heat, stirring frequently, until carrot is tender. Add bread crumbs and parsley; mix lightly. Spoon about 1 tablespoon stuffing on each fillet of flounder. Roll up fillets and place close together in shallow baking dish. Add water and 1 tablespoon of the sherry. Cover with aluminum foil and bake at 350°F. for 45 minutes, or until fish flakes easily. Drain fish and reserve 2 tablespoons of liquid from fish. Keep fish warm while making sauce. Add remaining 2 tablespoons sherry, the lemon juice and seasoned salt to fish stock in saucepan. Bring to boil and simmer 5 minutes. Beat in the butter and pour over flounder. Garnish with sliced olives. Makes 6 servings.

CALORIES PER SERVING 441
GRAMS OF PROTEIN PER SERVING 46
GRAMS OF CARBOHYDRATE PER SERVING 10
GRAMS OF FAT PER SERVING 21

Fish Steaks Tropical

 1 1/2 pounds halibut or haddock steaks
    2 teaspoons lemon juice
    1 teaspoon salt
 1/4 cup Spanish olive oil
    4 small bananas
 1/3 cup chopped, blanched almonds
    1 tablespoon chopped onion
 1/4 cup seedless raisins
    1 teaspoon minced parsley
    1 can (8 1/2 oz.) pineapple chunks, drained
 1/4 cup water
 1/4 cup Spanish sherry

Cut fish into serving pieces, sprinkle with lemon juice and salt. Heat olive oil in skillet. Saute fish gently on each side until delicately browned. Transfer to a shallow casserole. Peel bananas and slice lengthwise, saute in olive oil in skillet until lightly browned; remove and place around fish. Add the nuts and onion to skillet and cook one minute; add remaining ingredients, stirring well. Pour over fish in casserole. Bake at 325°F. for 15 minutes. Makes 4 servings.

CALORIES PER SERVING 527
GRAMS OF PROTEIN PER SERVING 39
GRAMS OF CARBOHYDRATE PER SERVING 41
GRAMS OF FAT PER SERVING 23

Rock Lobster Mexican Skillet

    3 packages (8 oz. each) rock lobster tails, thawed
      Salt and pepper
 1/2 cup lime juice
 1/4 cup Spanish olive oil
    2 scallions, chopped
 1/4 cup chopped green pepper
    1 can (28 oz.) tomatoes
 1/2 cup orange juice
 1 1/2 cups cooked rice
 1 1/2 cups cooked drained pinto or kidney beans
    2 tablespoons drained capers
 1/4 cup toasted slivered almonds

Cut away underside membrane of lobster tails with scissors. Remove raw meat from shells. Sprinkle meat with salt and pepper, and lime juice and let stand at room temperature about 20 minutes. Drain and rinse. Heat olive oil and saute scallions, and green pepper until tender. Add tomatoes, orange juice, rice and beans. When mixture simmers, add lobster. Cover tightly and simmer until lobster meat becomes opaque. Season to taste with salt and pepper. Garnish top with capers and slivered almonds. Serve with tortillas, if desired. Makes 6 servings.

CALORIES PER SERVING 452
GRAMS OF PROTEIN PER SERVING 34
GRAMS OF CARBOHYDRATE PER SERVING 45
GRAMS OF FAT PER SERVING 16

Fish with Orange Sauce

    2 pounds halibut fillets
    2 tablespoons Spanish olive oil
    1 tablespoon butter or margarine
    3 tablespoons minced onion
1 1/2 cups orange juice
    1 teaspoon grated orange rind
 1/2 cup dry white wine
 1/4 teaspoon salt
 1/8 teaspoon pepper

Saute fish in olive oil and butter until golden on one side; turn, add onion to olive oil around the fish, cook over moderate heat until onion is soft and the fish golden on the other side. Remove fish to platter. Add orange juice, rind, wine, salt and pepper to olive oil mixture in pan. Simmer 10 minutes. Return fish to pan; cook over moderate heat 10 minutes longer, or until flesh is firm. Serve fish with sauce. Makes 6 servings.

CALORIES PER SERVING 253
GRAMS OF PROTEIN PER SERVING 31
GRAMS OF CARBOHYDRATE PER SERVING 7
GRAMS OF FAT PER SERVING 8

Tuna Croquettes

    3 tablespoons Spanish olive oil
    3 tablespoons flour
 1/2 teaspoon salt
    1 tablespoon minced onion
    1 cup milk
    1 tablespoon lemon juice
    2 teaspoons Worcestershire sauce
    1 can (9 1/4 oz.) tuna, drained and flaked
1 1/2 cups soft bread crumbs
    1 egg, separated
    1 tablespoon Spanish olive oil
    1 cup dry bread crumbs

Heat 3 tablespoons olive oil in saucepan; blend in flour, salt and onion. Gradually stir in milk. Cook and stir over medium heat until thickened. Stir in lemon juice, Worcestershire sauce, tuna, soft bread crumbs; then egg yolk. Chill several hours. Form into 8 patties. Dip into egg white mixed with 1 tablespoon olive oil. Coat with dry crumbs. Place on greased baking sheet. Bake at 425°F. for 35 minutes. Makes 4 servings.

CALORIES PER SERVING 557
GRAMS OF PROTEIN PER SERVING 30
GRAMS OF CARBOHYDRATE PER SERVING 49
GRAMS OF FAT PER SERVING 25

Codfish in Spanish Tomato Sauce

    2 onions, chopped
    2 pimientos, diced
 1/4 cup Spanish olive oil
    1 can (15 oz.) tomato sauce
 1/2 teaspoon salt
 1/2 cup white wine
 1/2 cup minced parsley
    1 pound codfish

Slowly cook onion and pimiento in olive oil until very soft but not browned. Add tomato sauce, salt, wine and parsley; simmer at low heat for 30 minutes. If sauce thickens too much, add a little water. Add codfish, spooning sauce over fish, and simmer uncovered another 20 minutes or until fish flakes easily. Makes 3 servings.

CALORIES PER SERVING 546
GRAMS OF PROTEIN PER SERVING 30
GRAMS OF CARBOHYDRATE PER SERVING 24
GRAMS OF FAT PER SERVING 33

Halibut Mediterranean

2 pounds halibut
Water
Salt
2 slices lemon
2 slices onion
1 sprig of parsley
1/4 teaspoon peppercorns
3 large potatoes
3/4 pound green beans
3 carrots
3/4 cup Spanish olive oil
1/4 cup wine vinegar
2 tablespoons lemon juice
1 teaspoon salt
1/4 teaspoon freshly ground pepper
1/4 teaspoon dry mustard
1/4 teaspoon tarragon
1/8 teaspoon garlic salt
2 teaspoons chopped chives
Lettuce
Chopped parsley
2 tomatoes, quartered
3 hard-cooked eggs, quartered

To poach halibut, cover with boiling salted water. Add lemon and onion slices, a sprig of parsley and peppercorns. Cover and simmer 8 minutes or until halibut flakes when tested with a fork.

Cook potatoes in boiling, salted water until tender. Peel and slice. Snip ends from beans and cut in 1-inch pieces. Parboil until slightly tender, about 10 minutes; drain. Peel carrots. Cut in thin strips. Parboil until slightly tender, about 10 minutes; drain. Place halibut, potatoes, beans and carrots in 2 1/2 quart covered casserole. Combine olive oil, vinegar, lemon juice, salt, pepper, mustard, tarragon, garlic salt and chives. Pour over halibut and vegetables. Cover and refrigerate several hours. To serve, arrange halibut and vegetables on lettuce-lined platter. Sprinkle with chopped parsley and garnish with wedges of tomato and hard-cooked egg. Makes 6 servings.

CALORIES PER SERVING 530
GRAMS OF PROTEIN PER SERVING 37
GRAMS OF CARBOHYDRATE PER SERVING 21
GRAMS OF FAT PER SERVING 32

Salmon Teriyaki

4 salmon steaks
1/4 cup Sake
1/4 cup soy sauce
2 tablespoons Spanish olive oil
2 tablespoons sugar

Marinate the salmon steaks in Sake and soy sauce for 30 minutes at room temperature. Drain, reserving marinade. Heat olive oil in large skillet and saute salmon about five minutes on each side. Add sugar to marinade; pour over the salmon steaks. Lower heat, cover skillet and let simmer about 5 minutes until liquid is absorbed. Makes 4 servings.

CALORIES PER SERVING 144
GRAMS OF PROTEIN PER SERVING 6
GRAMS OF CARBOHYDRATE PER SERVING 4
GRAMS OF FAT PER SERVING 9

Scallops Marinera

1/4 cup Spanish olive oil
1 medium onion, chopped
1 small clove garlic, crushed
1/4 cup diced ham (optional)
1 pound scallops, fresh or frozen
1/4 teaspoon salt
1 pound clams in shell; or 1 can (7 oz.) minced clams
1/2 cup cider, dry white wine, or beer
1 tomato, peeled and chopped
1 tablespoon minced parsley
3 cups cooked rice
6 to 8 strips pimiento
2 hard-cooked eggs, quartered

Simmer onion, garlic and ham in olive oil until soft, about 10 minutes; add scallops and salt; cook about 3 minutes, turning once. Add clams (including juice of clams), cider, tomato and parsley. Cover and simmer 5 minutes or until clams open (if fresh clams are used). Arrange hot cooked rice around edge of shallow casserole; pour scallop-clam mixture in center. Garnish with strips of pimiento and hard-cooked egg wedges. Makes 6 servings.

CALORIES PER SERVING 328
GRAMS OF PROTEIN PER SERVING 24
GRAMS OF CARBOHYDRATE PER SERVING 27
GRAMS OF FAT PER SERVING 12

Mackerel and Macaroni Casserole

    1 package (8 oz.) macaroni
    2 medium sized onions, sliced
    1/2 pound mushrooms, sliced
    1/4 cup Spanish olive oil
    3 tablespoons flour
    1 cup milk
    1 teaspoon salt
    1/8 teaspoon white pepper
    2 tablespoons Sake
    1/4 cup grated Cheddar cheese
    2 tablespoons lemon juice
    1 can (6 1/2 oz.) mackerel, drained

Cook macaroni according to package directions, drain and set aside. Fry onion and mushrooms in 1 tablespoon olive oil for 10 minutes, stirring frequently, and set aside. Heat 3 tablespoons olive oil in a sauce pan; add flour. When the mixture starts to bubble, add milk little by little, stirring constantly. Add seasoning, Sake and cheese. Mix all the ingredients into the sauce, pour into buttered casserole and bake at 350°F. for 25-30 minutes. Makes 4 servings.

CALORIES PER SERVING 493
GRAMS OF PROTEIN PER SERVING 23
GRAMS OF CARBOHYDRATE PER SERVING 57
GRAMS OF FAT PER SERVING 17

Prawns in Salsa Verde

    1/2 cup Spanish olive oil
    3 cloves garlic, cut in half
    1 1/2 pounds large shrimp, shelled
    2 tablespoons flour
    1/2 cup Italian parsley, minced
    1/2 teaspoon salt, or to taste
    1/4 teaspoon powdered ginger
      Few grains pepper
    1 tablespoon monosodium glutamate
    2 tablespoons milk or cream
    1/2 or 3/4 cup water
    1/4 cup white wine
    4 hard-cooked eggs

Pour olive oil into heavy skillet, add garlic; saute until well-browned, then remove and set aside. Add shrimp, cover and cook 3 minutes until shrimp are pink. Remove shrimp and set aside. Mince the browned garlic, add to skillet with parsley and seasonings, blending well. Slowly add the milk or cream, then the water, a little at a time, and finally, the wine. Simmer until smooth and thickened. Add shrimp to the sauce, and simmer over low heat 5 minutes longer, shaking pan frequently. Serve with a garnish of hard-cooked eggs cut in wedges. Makes 6 servings.

CALORIES PER SERVING 393
GRAMS OF PROTEIN PER SERVING 26
GRAMS OF CARBOHYDRATE PER SERVING 15
GRAMS OF FAT PER SERVING 24

Crab Caribbean

    1 can (7 1/2 oz.) Alaska King crab or 1/2 lb.
      frozen Alaska King crab
    2 whole chicken breasts
    4 chicken legs
    3 tablespoons Spanish olive oil
    1 cup chopped onion
    1 cup uncooked rice
    4 cups chicken broth
    1 teaspoon salt
    1/4 teaspoon pepper
    1/8 teaspoon powdered saffron
    1/4 teaspoon tarragon
    1/4 teaspoon garlic powder
    2 ounces pimiento, sliced (about 1/4 cup)
    1 can (16 oz.) tomatoes
    1/2 cup sliced stuffed green olives
    1 package (10 oz.) frozen green peas

Drain crab and cut into bite-size pieces. Cut each chicken breast into 4 pieces. Saute chicken pieces in olive oil until golden brown, using Dutch oven or heavy kettle. Remove chicken. Add onion and saute until translucent. Add rice, chicken broth and seasonings. Cover and simmer 10 minutes. Add chicken, pimiento, tomatoes and olives. Simmer, covered, 10 minutes longer. Add crab and peas. Simmer about 5 minutes or just until peas are tender and crab is heated. Makes 6 servings.

CALORIES PER SERVING 410
GRAMS OF PROTEIN PER SERVING 44
GRAMS OF CARBOHYDRATE PER SERVING 29
GRAMS OF FAT PER SERVING 12

Rock Lobster Tails

    8 frozen rock lobster tails
    1/2 cup cider vinegar
    2/3 cup Spanish olive oil
    2 teaspoons salt
    1/2 teaspoon white pepper
    1/2 cup minced onion
    1 1/2 cups unsweetened pineapple juice

Take frozen tails and cut down through middle of hard shell with sharp knife. Grasp tail in both hands and open flat butterfly style. Combine all other ingredients and beat until well blended. Place rock lobster tail shellside down in a shallow pan. Pour marinade over the tails and let stand until they are defrosted. When coals are hot, grill tails for 5 minutes, flesh side towards heat. Turn, brush flesh with marinade. Grill flesh side up until meat has lost its transparency and is opaque. Brush tails with sauce several times during cooking, and before serving. Serves 4.

CALORIES PER SERVING 567
GRAMS OF PROTEIN PER SERVING 34
GRAMS OF CARBOHYDRATE PER SERVING 16
GRAMS OF FAT PER SERVING 40

Clams Marinera

    1 quart cherrystone clams in shell or 1 can
       (10 oz.) whole clams, drained
    2 to 3 cloves garlic, minced
    2 pimientos, chopped
    1/2 cup chopped onion
    1/4 cup Spanish olive oil
    1/2 cup drained canned tomatoes or
       tomato sauce
    2 tablespoons sherry
    1/4 cup chopped parlsey
       Salt and pepper to taste

Drain clams, reserving 1/4 cup of the liquid. Saute garlic, pimiento and onion in olive oil in skillet until tender. Add tomatoes, sherry and the reserved clam liquid. Cook over medium heat 3 to 4 minutes, stirring occasionally. Add clams, cook 4 minutes (or until shells have opened). Add parsley during last minute. Season to taste. Serve clams hot with only 1/2 cup of the cooking liquid, reserving remainder for dip. Makes 6 servings.

Marinera Dip

    Reserved sauce from above recipe
    3 tablespoons flour
    3 tablespoons cold water

Return sauce to skillet in which the clams were prepared. In a small bowl, combine the flour and water; mix to a smooth paste, stir in a little of the sauce. Blend well, and pour into skillet. Stirring constantly, bring sauce to a slow boil; remove from heat. Blend at medium speed of blender 1 minute. Serve hot or cold as a dip for clams or cubes of crusty French or Italian bread. Makes 1 1/2 cups.

CALORIES PER SERVING 196
GRAMS OF PROTEIN PER SERVING 9
GRAMS OF CARBOHYDRATE PER SERVING 9
GRAMS OF FAT PER SERVING 12

Rock Lobster in Marinade

    3 packages (8 oz. each) frozen rock lobster
       tails
    3 medium onions, thinly sliced
    1 lemon, cut into thin slices
    1/2 cup chopped parsley
    1 teaspoon salt
    1/4 teaspoon white pepper
    1/4 teaspoon Tabasco sauce
    2 bay leaves
    1/2 cup Spanish olive oil

Parboil frozen rock lobster tails by dropping into boiling salted water. When water reboils, drain immediately and drench with cold water. With scissors, remove underside membrane and pull out meat in one piece. Cut lobster meat into halves lengthwise. Combine lobster meat with remaining ingredients and toss, adding enough olive oil to cover mixture. Cover and marinate 6 to 8 hours in refrigerator. Serve cold with thin slices of pumpernickel bread, if desired. Makes 6 servings.

CALORIES PER SERVING 290
GRAMS OF PROTEIN PER SERVING 7
GRAMS OF CARBOHYDRATE PER SERVING 6
GRAMS OF FAT PER SERVING 27

Spanish Salmon Steaks with Olives

   4 salmon steaks, about 2 pounds
1/4 cup Spanish olive oil
 12 pimiento-stuffed olives
1/2 cup finely chopped onion
   1 tablespoon minced parsley
1/2 teaspoon salt
   1 tablespoon wine vinegar
1/2 cup clam juice
     Amarilla Sauce

Select a covered baking dish that will hold the 4 steaks in a single layer, about 10-inch square or 11 x 7. In bottom of dish place half of the olive oil, and cover evenly with olives, onion and parsley. Sprinkle with salt. Top with salmon steaks. Mix remaining oil with vinegar and clam juice and pour over all. Cover and bake at 325°F. for 30 minutes. Use pancake turner or spatula to lift steaks from baking pan, and turn steaks over as they are placed on serving platter. Spoon drippings from pan over steaks. Serve with Amarilla Sauce. Makes 4 servings.

Amarilla Sauce

   6 hard-cooked eggs
   2 tablespoons Spanish olive oil
   2 tablespoons Spanish cream sherry
1/2 teaspoon salt
1/2 teaspoon dry mustard
     Dash pepper
   1 tablespoon wine vinegar

Place ingredients in electric blender and whirl until smooth. (Or sieve eggs and mix with remaining ingredients.)

CALORIES PER SERVING 834
GRAMS OF PROTEIN PER SERVING 78
GRAMS OF CARBOHYDRATE PER SERVING 6
GRAMS OF FAT PER SERVING 49

POULTRY

Chicken Stew

- 1 cup onion flakes
- 1 teaspoon instant minced garlic
- 3/4 cup water
- 2 tablespoons Spanish olive oil
- 1 chicken, about 3 pounds, cut into eighths
- 1 pound beef cubes, cut into 1 inch pieces
- 1/2 pound pork sausage links, cut in half
- 2 tablespoons flour
- 1 can (20 oz.) chick peas
- 1 can (16 oz.) tomatoes, broken up
- 1 can (16 oz.) whole potatoes
- 1/4 cup celery flakes
- 2 tablespoons parsley flakes
- 2 1/2 teaspoons salt
- 2 teaspoons paprika
- 1/2 teaspoon crushed red pepper
- 1/2 pound cooked ham, cubed
- 1 package (10 oz.) frozen peas

Mix onion flakes and minced garlic in water; let stand 10 minutes to rehydrate. Heat olive oil in a Dutch oven or large heavy pot. Add chicken, beef and sausage, a few pieces at a time; brown well, removing and setting aside when browned. Pour off all but 2 tablespoons oil. Add rehydrated onion and garlic to oil in pot; saute 5 minutes. Stir in flour. Drain liquids from canned chick peas, tomatoes and potatoes; add enough water to measure 2 quarts; stir into flour, onions and garlic. Return chicken and beef to pot. Add tomatoes, potatoes, celery flakes, parsley flakes, salt, paprika and red pepper. Cover and simmer until chicken is almost tender, about 25 minutes. Add reserved sausage, ham, chick peas and peas. Cook until vegetables and meat are tender. Makes 8 servings.

```
CALORIES PER SERVING ............................. 522
GRAMS OF PROTEIN PER SERVING .................... 51
GRAMS OF CARBOHYDRATE PER SERVING ........... 21
GRAMS OF FAT PER SERVING ........................ 24
```

Orange Glazed Chicken

- 1/2 cup Spanish olive oil
- 1/2 cup orange juice
- 1 tablespoon wine vinegar
- 1 teaspoon salt
- 1 teaspoon instant chopped onion
- 1/4 teaspoon ginger or cumin
- 1 chicken, about 3 pounds

Combine olive oil, juice, vinegar and salt; crush the instant onion with mortar and pestle or back of wooden spoon, blend with the ginger or cumin. Add to the juice mixture. Marinate either whole or cut-up chicken in the sauce for 1 hour or longer; baste with the marinade as it cooks over charcoal or in the broiler or rotisserie oven. Makes 1 cup sauce.

```
CALORIES PER SERVING ............................. 2408
GRAMS OF PROTEIN PER SERVING ................... 182
GRAMS OF CARBOHYDRATE PER SERVING ...........  13
GRAMS OF FAT PER SERVING ....................... 177
```

Barbecued Chicken with Sherry Marinade

- 1/4 cup Spanish olive oil
- 2 tablespoons soy sauce
- 1 cup dry sherry
- 1/2 teaspoon oregano
- 1 chicken, about 3 pounds, whole or cut up

Combine olive oil, soy sauce, sherry, and oregano; pour over chicken and refrigerate 6 to 12 hours, turning several times. Remove chicken from marinade. Place whole chicken on rotisserie spit and cook, basting frequently with marinade for 1 to 1 1/4 hours over medium-hot fire, until leg moves very easily. Place cut-up chicken on flat grill; turn and baste frequently until pieces are well-browned on both sides. If roasted on electric rotisserie, or broiled save drippings and serve as unthickened gravy with the chicken. Makes 4 servings.

```
CALORIES PER SERVING ............................. 551
GRAMS OF PROTEIN PER SERVING ....................  45
GRAMS OF CARBOHYDRATE PER SERVING ...........   5
GRAMS OF FAT PER SERVING ......................... 30
```

Chicken a la Praviana

  1 frying chicken, about 3 pounds, cut up
1/4 cup Spanish olive oil
1/4 pound ham, diced (about 1/2 cup)
  1 medium onion, chopped
  1 or 2 cloves garlic, minced
1/2 cup cider, white wine or beer
  1 tablespoon minced parsley
3/4 teaspoon salt (or to taste)
1/2 pound shelled large shrimp
    Dash of paprika

Saute the chicken pieces in olive oil until crisply-browned and tender, about 35 minutes. (To prevent oil from spattering, add a few slices of onion to the oil.) Set chicken aside. Add ham, onion and garlic, simmer in olive oil over moderate heat until onion is soft. Replace chicken; add cider, parsley, salt and the uncooked shrimp. Cover, cook over lowest heat until shrimp are bright pink, about 7 minutes. Serve with rice. May be garnished with triangles of bread which have been fried until crisp in olive oil. Makes 6 servings.

CALORIES PER SERVING 387
GRAMS OF PROTEIN PER SERVING 39
GRAMS OF CARBOHYDRATE PER SERVING 3
GRAMS OF FAT PER SERVING 21

Fried Chicken Oriental

  2 chicken breasts, boned and split
1/2 teaspoon salt
    Pinch of black pepper
  2 tablespoons Sake
1/4 cup cornstarch
1/4 cup Spanish olive oil

Cut the chicken breasts into bite-size pieces. Season with salt and pepper, sprinkle with Sake and let stand for 20 minutes. Thinly coat the chicken pieces with the cornstarch. Heat the olive oil in a large frying pan and fry the chicken quickly until golden brown. Turn the heat to very low, cover the pan and let simmer for three minutes more. Makes 4 servings.

CALORIES PER SERVING 267
GRAMS OF PROTEIN PER SERVING 23
GRAMS OF CARBOHYDRATE PER SERVING 7
GRAMS OF FAT PER SERVING 14

Chicken a la Tenerife

  1 chicken, about 3 pounds, cut up
1/4 cup flour
  1 teaspoon salt
1/2 cup Spanish olive oil
  2 cloves garlic, minced
  1 small onion, minced
1/8 teaspoon cinnamon
1/8 teaspoon cloves
  2 cups white wine
    Salt to taste

Dust chicken pieces in flour mixed with salt; fry in olive oil over moderate heat until very brown and crisp. (Place piece of bread or slices of onion in oil to prevent spattering.) Remove chicken from skillet. Pour off all but 2 tablespoons of the olive oil. Add garlic, onion, cinnamon, and cloves; saute until onion is soft. Add white wine, simmer 10 minutes. Add salt if needed. Return chicken to skillet and spoon sauce over chicken. Simmer gently about 20 minutes until chicken is very tender. Makes 4 servings.

CALORIES PER SERVING 711
GRAMS OF PROTEIN PER SERVING 46
GRAMS OF CARBOHYDRATE PER SERVING 10
GRAMS OF FAT PER SERVING 44

Fiji Orange Chicken Chunks

6 whole chicken breasts, boned, skinned and
    cut into 2-inch pieces
1½ teaspoons garlic salt
1 teaspoon paprika
¼ cup Spanish olive oil
1 can (9 oz.) pineapple chunks
1¼ cups chicken broth
¼ cup wine vinegar
½ cup sliced celery
1 small green pepper, cut into ¼-inch strips
1 large onion, sliced
1 large tomato, cut into wedges
1 tablespoon soy sauce
3 tablespoons dark brown sugar
2 tablespoons cornstarch
½ cup water
3 oranges, sectioned
4 cups fried rice

Sprinkle chicken pieces with garlic salt and paprika. Heat olive oil in large skillet; add chicken and cook about 5 minutes. Drain syrup from pineapple. Add syrup, chicken broth and vinegar to chicken. Cover and simmer 10 minutes. Add celery, green pepper and onion. Cover and cook 5 minutes longer. Add tomato wedges and drained pineapple chunks. Blend soy sauce, brown sugar, cornstarch and water. Add to skillet and cook, stirring constantly, until mixture thickens and comes to a boil; cook 1 minute longer. Add orange sections and toss lightly. Serve over fried rice. Makes 6 servings.

```
CALORIES PER SERVING ......................... 514
GRAMS OF PROTEIN PER SERVING ............... 51
GRAMS OF CARBOHYDRATE PER SERVING ........... 50
GRAMS OF FAT PER SERVING ..................... 11
```

Roman Style Chicken with White Sauce

1 chicken, about 2½ to 3 pounds
2 tablespoons Spanish olive oil
½ teaspoon powdered cumin
½ teaspoon salt
1 leek or 2 scallions, chopped
1 sprig celery leaves, minced
1½ cups water
1 tablespoon soy sauce
½ cup light cream
1 egg white, beaten

Brush inside of chicken with a mixture of the olive oil, cumin and salt. Place chopped leek and celery leaves in cavity; truss. Place in basket or on rack, with water in bottom of Dutch oven or electric skillet. Rub soy sauce over chicken. Cover pan tightly, bring just to a boil and reduce heat as low as possible. Simmer or steam for 1½ hours or until leg moves easily. Remove chicken. Add cream to liquid in pan, heat and stir; add a little of the hot sauce to beaten egg white, blend well, combine with remaining sauce and cook over very low heat until thickened. Serve sauce with chicken. Makes 4 servings.

```
CALORIES PER SERVING ......................... 366
GRAMS OF PROTEIN PER SERVING ............... 32
GRAMS OF CARBOHYDRATE PER SERVING ........... 3
GRAMS OF FAT PER SERVING ..................... 24
```

Onion Sauced Chicken

6 tablespoons flour
1½ teaspoons salt
¼ teaspoon pepper
1 chicken, about 3 pounds, cut up
¼ cup Spanish olive oil
1 sweet Spanish onion sliced
3 tablespoons flour
1½ cups chicken stock or bouillon
½ teaspoon salt
    Dash pepper
¼ teaspoon thyme

Combine 6 tablespoons flour, 1½ teaspoons salt and ¼ teaspoon pepper in paper or plastic bag. Add 2 or 3 pieces of chicken at a time and shake until coated with flour mixture. Brown chicken in olive oil. Place in 2-quart casserole. Saute sliced onion in chicken drippings until golden. Add 3 tablespoons flour and stir until blended. Add chicken stock and cook until thickened. Season with remaining salt, pepper and thyme. Pour over chicken. Cover and bake at 350°F. for 1¼ hours or until chicken is tender. Makes 4 servings.

```
CALORIES PER SERVING ......................... 541
GRAMS OF PROTEIN PER SERVING ............... 49
GRAMS OF  CARBOHYDRATE PER SERVING ........... 14
GRAMS OF FAT PER SERVING ..................... 30
```

Chicken Ragout

1½ cups white wine
1 can (4 oz.) mushroom buttons, drained
½ cup chopped celery
½ cup chopped onion
½ cup thinly sliced carrots
1 teaspoon salt
½ teaspoon pepper
½ teaspoon thyme
¼ teaspoon ground cinnamon
¼ teaspoon ground cloves
1 bay leaf
1 clove garlic, minced
4 pounds chicken breasts or pieces
¼ cup Spanish olive oil
¼ cup flour
1 package (3 oz.) smoked, sliced dried beef, torn in pieces
2 packages (8 oz. each) medium noodles, cooked and drained
½ cup grated Parmesan cheese
Sour cream

Combine wine, mushrooms, celery, onion, carrots and spices in small saucepan and warm slightly. Pour mixture over chicken and marinate 2 hours or overnight in refrigerator. Brown chicken in olive oil; remove from pan. Stir flour into olive oil and cook until very brown. Add marinade and stir until smooth. Add chicken and dried beef; cover and cook 1 hour. Toss hot noodles with cheese. Serve chicken and sauce over noodles. Garnish with sour cream. Makes 8 servings.

CALORIES PER SERVING 679
GRAMS OF PROTEIN PER SERVING 69
GRAMS OF CARBOHYDRATE PER SERVING 47
GRAMS OF FAT PER SERVING 17

Pear-Chicken Bake

1 can (16 oz.) pear halves
1 chicken, about 2½ pounds, cut up
Salt and pepper
3 tablespoons Spanish olive oil
1 medium onion, sliced
3 tablespoons flour
½ teaspoon basil
¾ cup water
⅓ cup dry white wine
1 cup halved cherry tomatoes

Drain and quarter pears, reserving ⅓ cup syrup. Sprinkle chicken pieces with salt and pepper. Brown chicken in olive oil in skillet. Remove to casserole. Saute sliced onion until tender in remaining oil in skillet. Blend in flour and basil. Add water gradually, cooking and stirring until thickened and bubbly. Add reserved ⅓ cup pear syrup and white wine. Add pears and tomatoes and cook for a few minutes longer. Season to taste with salt and pepper. Pour pear sauce over chicken in casserole. Cover and bake at 350°F. for 45 minutes, or until chicken in tender, removing cover for last 5 minutes. Serve with parslied rice or pilaf, as desired. Makes 4 servings.

CALORIES PER SERVING 467
GRAMS OF PROTEIN PER SERVING 39
GRAMS OF CARBOHYDRATE PER SERVING 19
GRAMS OF FAT PER SERVING 24

Blueberry Stuffed Cornish Game Hens

8 cornish game hens, thawed
Salt and pepper
¼ cup Spanish olive oil
¼ cup lemon juice
¼ cup aromatic bitters
4 cups fresh or frozen dry-pack blueberries
4 teaspoons sugar
½ cup butter or margarine
8 small bay leaves

Sprinkle game hens inside and out with salt and pepper. Mix olive oil, lemon juice and bitters, and brush game hens with mixture inside and out. Fill each bird with ½ cup blueberries and ½ teaspoon sugar. Sew or skewer openings and place on a shallow roasting pan. Spread soft butter over breasts of birds and place bay leaf on butter. Roast in a preheated oven at 350°F. for 1 hour or until legs move easily. Serve garnished with additional blueberries. Makes 8 servings.

CALORIES PER SERVING 442
GRAMS OF PROTEIN PER SERVING 30
GRAMS OF CARBOHYDRATE PER SERVING 13
GRAMS OF FAT PER SERVING 29

Roast Stuffed Chicken

1/2 cup Spanish olive oil
3/4 cup chopped celery
1/2 cup chopped onion
  4 cups dry bread cubes
  1 teaspoon salt
1/2 teaspoon thyme
1/2 teaspoon sage
1/2 teaspoon marjoram
1/8 teaspoon pepper
  1 roasting chicken, 4 to 5 pounds
  1 teaspoon salt
    Additional Spanish olive oil

Heat olive oil in large skillet; saute celery and onion until tender, but not browned. Add bread cubes, 1 teaspoon salt and seasonings; heat until lightly browned and oil is absorbed by bread cubes. Cool thoroughly. Sprinkle neck and body cavities with 1 teaspoon salt. Stuff with prepared stuffing. Hook wing tips onto back to hold neck skin. Tie legs together; then tie to tail. Place chicken directly into shallow pan (no rack is necessary). Brush with olive oil. Roast at 375°F. for 2 1/4 to 2 3/4 hours. To test for doneness, drumstick meat should feel soft when pressed between fingers and leg should twist easily out of thigh joint. Makes 6 servings.

CALORIES PER SERVING 747
GRAMS OF PROTEIN PER SERVING 48
GRAMS OF CARBOHYDRATE PER SERVING 45
GRAMS OF FAT PER SERVING 40

Chicken in Beer Gravy

    3 pounds chicken pieces
    2 tablespoons Spanish olive oil
1/3 cup flour
    1 teaspoon salt
1/4 teaspoon pepper
    1 envelope onion soup mix
    1 can (12 oz.) beer or cola

Coat chicken pieces with a mixture of flour, salt, and pepper. Brown in olive oil in pressure cooker. Mix any remaining seasoned flour with the soup mix. When chicken is brown, pile it to one side of the cooker; stir the soup mix and beer into the drippings. Stir until blended. Place chicken pieces evenly over bottom of pan. Close cover securely. Place pressure regulator on vent pipe. Cook for 15 minutes. Cool cooker at once. Makes 6 servings.

```
CALORIES PER SERVING ............................. 341
GRAMS OF PROTEIN PER SERVING ................... 32
GRAMS OF CARBOHYDRATE PER SERVING ........... 10
GRAMS OF FAT PER SERVING ....................... 16
```

Chicken Casserole

    1 cup chicken stock
    1 chicken, about 3 pounds, cut up
1/2 teaspoon salt
1/4 cup Spanish olive oil
    6 blanched almonds
    2 strips bacon, diced
    1 medium onion, chopped fine
    2 garlic cloves, crushed
    1 can (4 oz.) pimientoes, drained, diced
    1 teaspoon tomato puree or catsup
1/4 cup medium dry sherry

Make chicken stock by cooking neck, giblets and wing tips in 2 cups salted water for 1/2 hour. Strain liquid. Meantime, dust remaining chicken parts with salt. In frying pan, heat olive oil; brown chicken over moderate heat and remove from pan. Add blanched almonds, brown lightly; remove. Add bacon, onion, garlic, and pimiento and cook until onion is soft. Add remaining ingredients, chicken stock and chicken. Simmer until chicken is tender, about 45 minutes. Top with almonds to serve. Makes 4 servings.

```
CALORIES PER SERVING ............................. 531
GRAMS OF PROTEIN PER SERVING ................... 47
GRAMS OF CARBOHYDRATE PER SERVING ........... 5
GRAMS OF FAT PER SERVING ....................... 32
```

Oven-Barbecued Turkey

    2 small turkeys (4 pounds each)
    1 or 2 cloves of garlic
      Water

Split turkeys into halves or quarters, or disjoint and cut into serving pieces or buy cut-up turkey parts. Place turkey skin-side down in shallow pan. Add 1 or 2 garlic cloves. Pour in water to fill pan about 3/4 inch. Bake at 375°F. for 1 hour, turning pieces of turkey occasionally. Water should be reduced during cooking to just cover bottom of pan. Meanwhile prepare the barbecue sauce.

Barbecue Sauce

    1 teaspoon sugar
1/4 teaspoon dry mustard
    2 teaspoons salt
1/4 teaspoon black pepper
    2 tablespoons Worcestershire sauce
    2 cups tomato juice
1/2 cup lemon juice or vinegar
1/4 cup Spanish olive oil

Mix sugar, mustard, salt and pepper in saucepan. Add Worcestershire sauce, tomato juice, lemon juice and olive oil. Heat to boiling and pour sauce over partially cooked turkey. Continue cooking, turning the pieces of turkey occasionally. Baste frequently with the sauce from the bottom of the pan, leaving a pool of sauce in rib cage when halves are turned up. Cook until turkey is tender and sauce is reduced to a rich gravy, about 1 to 1 1/2 hours longer. If sauce thickens before turkey is done, add 1/2 to 1 cup boiling water. Lift turkey to hot platter. Serve the sauce separately. For a brown crustiness, place well-basted turkey skin-side up under broiler. Makes 12 servings.

```
CALORIES PER SERVING ............................. 253
GRAMS OF PROTEIN PER SERVING ................... 31
GRAMS OF CARBOHYDRATE PER SERVING ........... 3
GRAMS OF FAT PER SERVING ....................... 12
```

Vegetables:

Often a challenge . . . to make them interesting to eat
. . . vegetables take on a new lease on life when Spanish
olive oil is used. It's important to make this nutritious
part of the meal appealing to all.

Ratatouille
(Vegetables Provencale)

1/3 cup Spanish olive oil
2 cloves garlic, crushed
1 large onion, sliced into thick rings
4 medium zucchini, sliced
1 medium eggplant, peeled and diced
1 green pepper, seeds removed, cut into rings
4 firm medium tomatoes, quartered
2 teaspoons salt
1/2 teaspoon pepper
1/2 cup black olives (optional)

Heat olive oil in skillet, saute garlic and
onion a few seconds. Add remaining vegetables except olives; saute about 15 minutes
until tender, turning occasionally to cook
thoroughly. Serve hot or cold garnished
with olives, as an accompaniment or an appetizer. Makes 10 servings.

CALORIES PER SERVING 132
GRAMS OF PROTEIN PER SERVING 2
GRAMS OF CARBOHYDRATE PER SERVING 10
GRAMS OF FAT PER SERVING 9

Baked Eggplant in Foil

1 medium eggplant (do not peel), cut into
   cubes
2 teaspoons onion powder
1/2 teaspoon salt
1 teaspoon minced parsley
1/3 cup Spanish olive oil
1/3 cup canned tomato sauce

Place cubes of eggplant on a large piece of
foil. Sprinkle with onion powder, salt, minced parsley, olive oil and tomato sauce.
Wrap foil securely to cover. Place bundle
over charcoal and cook until eggplant is
very tender, about 1 hour (depending on
heat of fire). Makes 6 servings.

CALORIES PER SERVING 154
GRAMS OF PROTEIN PER SERVING 1
GRAMS OF CARBOHYDRATE PER SERVING 7
GRAMS OF FAT PER SERVING 13

Fassoli Fresca

1/4 cup Spanish olive oil
1/2 cup chopped onion
1 clove garlic, minced
2 cups cut green beans
1 cup cooked lima beans
1 cup peeled and chopped whole tomatoes
2 tablespoons minced parsley
   Salt to taste

In a skillet, heat olive oil; saute onions and
garlic until tender. Add remaining ingredients. Simmer, uncovered, for 8 to 10
minutes or until beans are just tender.
Makes 4 servings.

CALORIES PER SERVING 215
GRAMS OF PROTEIN PER SERVING 5
GRAMS OF CARBOHYDRATE PER SERVING 18
GRAMS OF FAT PER SERVING 14

Baked Stuffed Squash

    4   zucchini (6 to 8 inches long)
  1/4   cup Spanish olive oil
  1/2   cup coarse bread crumbs
    1   pound ground lamb
    2   cloves garlic, minced
    1   tablespoon chopped parsley
    1   teaspoon salt
    1   can (10 3/4 oz.) condensed cream of
          mushroom soup
    1   teaspoon paprika
  1/4   cup white wine or broth
          Few drops of almond extract

Boil squash in boiling salted water 10 minutes. Drain, cut in half lengthwise, and scoop out centers. Place zucchini shells in shallow baking dish. Saute bread crumbs in olive oil until golden brown. Drain on absorbent paper and set aside to sprinkle on top of stuffed squash. In olive oil remaining in skillet, brown lamb with garlic, parsley, salt and centers scooped from squash. Spoon into squash shells. Mix soup with paprika, wine, and almond extract. Spoon over squash. Sprinkle with sauteed crumbs. Bake at 350°F. for 45 minutes. Makes 4 servings.

CALORIES PER SERVING 394
GRAMS OF PROTEIN PER SERVING 18
GRAMS OF CARBOHYDRATE PER SERVING 20
GRAMS OF FAT PER SERVING 24

Savory Baked Tomatoes

    4   large tomatoes
  1/3   cup Spanish olive oil
    1   small onion, chopped
    1   pimiento, cut into strips
    2   tablespoons minced ham
  1/2   teaspoons salt
  1/8   teaspoon pepper
  1/4   teaspoon marjoram
    1   tablespoon minced parsley
    1   cup soft bread crumbs

Cut a 2-inch wide cap from the stem end of the tomatoes. Hollow out tomatoes, removing pulp and discard with the caps. Heat 4 tablespoons of olive oil in a skillet, add onion, and saute until tender. Stir in remaining ingredients, browning slightly.

Spoon stuffing mixture into tomatoes. Place remaining 2 tablespoons olive oil into a shallow baking pan, arrange stuffed tomatoes in the pan, brush with a little of the oil. Bake at 350°F. for 40 minutes until cooked through. Makes 4 servings.

CALORIES PER SERVING 319
GRAMS OF PROTEIN PER SERVING 6
GRAMS OF CARBOHYDRATE PER SERVING 28
GRAMS OF FAT PER SERVING 20

Spinach Lasagne

  3/4   cup finely chopped onion
    1   clove garlic, minced
    2   tablespoons Spanish olive oil
    1   pound ground beef
    1   can (8 oz.) tomato sauce
    1   can (6 oz.) tomato paste
  3/4   cup water
    1   can (1 3/4 oz.) sliced mushrooms
    1   teaspoon Italian seasoning
    2   teaspoons salt
    1   egg, beaten
    1   package (10 oz.) frozen chopped spinach,
          thawed
    2   cups cream style cottage cheese
  1/3   cup grated Parmesan cheese
    1   package (12 oz.) lasagne noodles, cooked
          and drained
    8   ounces Mozzarella cheese, sliced

Saute onion and garlic in olive oil in large skillet. Add ground beef and cook until brown. Add tomato sauce, tomato paste, water, mushrooms with liquid, Italian seasoning and 1 teaspoon salt. Simmer uncovered, 15 to 20 minutes. Meanwhile, combine beaten egg, spinach, cottage cheese, Parmesan cheese and remaining 1 teaspoon salt. Pour half of meat sauce in 9 x 13-inch baking pan. Cover with layer of lasagne, half the spinach mixture, another layer of lasagne and half the cheese slices. Repeat layers. Cover and bake at 375°F. for 30 minutes. Uncover and bake an additional 10 minutes. Cut in squares to serve. Makes 8 servings.

CALORIES PER SERVING 414
GRAMS OF PROTEIN PER SERVING 31
GRAMS OF CARBOHYDRATE PER SERVING 12
GRAMS OF FAT PER SERVING 26

Garbanzos

1 or 2 cloves garlic
2 tablespoons Spanish olive oil
1 medium onion, thinly sliced
2 pimientos, chopped
1 can (20 oz.) garbanzos (chick peas),
   drained
1/4 teaspoon salt
1/4 cup minced parsley
   Freshly ground black pepper

Brown the whole garlic in the olive oil;
remove garlic and discard. Add onion and
pimiento; cook until onion is soft. Add garbanzos, salt, parsley and pepper; cover and
simmer over lowest heat for 5 to 10 minutes. Makes 4 servings.

CALORIES PER SERVING 434
GRAMS OF PROTEIN PER SERVING 21
GRAMS OF CARBOHYDRATE PER SERVING 63
GRAMS OF FAT PER SERVING 11

Marinated Roasted Red Peppers

6 red peppers, roasted, peeled and trimmed
1 cup Spanish olive oil
1/2 cup white wine vinegar
1 clove garlic, minced or mashed
1/2 teaspoon salt
1/2 teaspoon oregano
1/2 teaspoon basil
1/4 teaspoon pepper

Cut roasted red peppers into half-inch
strips. Combine with rest of ingredients in a
bowl. Cover and refrigerate several hours
or up to a week. Makes 4 cups.

Roasting Instructions

To roast red peppers over a gas burner, use
a pronged fork to hold pepper an inch
above highest gas flame. To roast under a
broiler, arrange 3 or 4 peppers on a broiler
pan and place an inch below a preheated
broiler. Turn peppers until evenly blistered
and charred. As each pepper is blistered,
drop into a plastic bag; close top and let
cool. Remove one pepper at a time and pull
off all peel with a knife; cut in half, remove
stems, seeds, and membrane. To freeze,
pack roasted, peeled, and cut peppers in
freezer containers; cover and freeze. Thaw
at room temperature or in refrigerator. You
can refrigerate thawed peppers up to 3 days.

Serving suggestions:

Mix diced or thinly sliced peppers with
some of the marinade into macaroni,
potato, or green salads.

Add thin marinated pepper strips to pizza
toppings before baking.

Pile wide strips of marinated peppers on
cheeseburgers or open-faced sandwiches
before serving (or top cheese sandwiches
with strips before toasting).

Include on antipasto platters.

CALORIES PER SERVING 526
GRAMS OF PROTEIN PER SERVING 1
GRAMS OF CARBOHYDRATE PER SERVING 7
GRAMS OF FAT PER SERVING 56

Braised Zucchini

1 1/2 pounds zucchini
2 medium onions, sliced
6 tablespoons Spanish olive oil
1 can (16 oz.) tomatoes
2 tablespoons minced parsley; or 1 teaspoon
   minced dill
1 teaspoon salt
   Dash of pepper

Cut squash into 2-inch pieces. Cook onions
in olive oil until golden but not browned;
add squash, tomatoes, parsley, salt and pepper. Simmer, uncovered, about 30 minutes.
Serve hot or cold. Makes 6 servings.

CALORIES PER SERVING 175
GRAMS OF PROTEIN PER SERVING 2
GRAMS OF CARBOHYDRATE PER SERVING 11
GRAMS OF FAT PER SERVING 14

Austrian Cheese-Stuffed Cauliflower

    1 large head of cauliflower, trimmed and left
       whole
    4 ounces Austrian Swiss Cheese, cut length-
       wise (1-inch thick)
       Salt and freshly ground pepper to taste
 1/4 cup Spanish olive oil
    1 cup finely crushed stuffing mix

Cook cauliflower in boiling salted water until tender, but still firm. Drain. Place whole head in shallow baking pan. Press sticks of Swiss cheese into cauliflower all over head. Sprinkle with salt and pepper. Mix olive oil and stuffing and press mixture onto the cauliflower. Bake at 350°F. for 20 minutes, or until crumbs are lightly browned. Arrange on platter garnished with tomato slices and parsley or watercress, if desired. Cut in wedges to serve. Makes 6 servings.

CALORIES PER SERVING 309
GRAMS OF PROTEIN PER SERVING 13
GRAMS OF CARBOHYDRATE PER SERVING 31
GRAMS OF FAT PER SERVING 16

Austrian Green Bean Casserole

    2 package frozen green beans, cooked and
       drained
    1 large onion, chopped
 1/4 cup Spanish olive oil
 1/4 cup flour
    1 cup light cream
    1 cup milk
    2 envelopes dehydrated chicken broth
       Salt and freshly ground pepper to taste
    1 cup grated Austrian Swiss cheese
    1 can French fried onions.

Cool green beans. In a saucepan, saute onion in olive oil for 5 minutes or until tender. Stir in flour. Gradually mix in cream, milk and chicken broth. Stir over low heat until sauce bubbles and thickens. Season with salt and pepper. Add cheese, stir until melted. Add green beans and pour into a 1 1/2 quart casserole. Sprinkle with fried onions. Bake at 350°F. for 30 minutes. Makes 8 servings.

CALORIES PER SERVING 248
GRAMS OF PROTEIN PER SERVING 8
GRAMS OF CARBOHYDRATE PER SERVING 12
GRAMS OF FAT PER SERVING 19

Parsley Sauce

    1 cup minced parsley
    1 clove garlic, minced
 1/4 cup Spanish olive oil
 1/4 teaspoon salt
 1/8 teaspoon pepper
    1 tablespoon vinegar

Mash minced parsley and garlic using a mortar and pestle or an electric blender; slowly add olive oil. Add salt, pepper and vinegar to taste. Serve over hot cooked vegetables. Makes 4 servings.

CALORIES PER SERVING 130
GRAMS OF PROTEIN PER SERVING 0
GRAMS OF CARBOHYDRATE PER SERVING 1
GRAMS OF FAT PER SERVING 14

Salsa Verde
(Spanish Green Sauce)

1/4 cup Spanish olive oil
2 cloves garlic
1/2 cup parsley, minced
2 tablespoons flour
1/2 teaspoon salt
1/4 teaspoon powdered ginger
    Few grains pepper
2 tablespoons milk or light cream
1/2 cup water
1/4 cup white wine

Pour olive oil in skillet; add garlic, saute until golden, then remove. Mash garlic with parsley using a mortar and pestle; add flour, salt, ginger and pepper, blend well. Return to pan; slowly add milk, then the water. Cook and stir over medium heat until thickened; add wine. Serve over cooked vegetables. Makes 6 servings.

CALORIES PER SERVING 110
GRAMS OF PROTEIN PER SERVING 0
GRAMS OF CARBOHYDRATE PER SERVING 3
GRAMS OF FAT PER SERVING 9

Almond and Hot Pepper Sauce

2 egg yolks or 1 whole egg
1/4 cup toasted almonds
1 clove garlic
1/4 teaspoon cayenne pepper
1 teaspoon salt
1 small tomato, peeled and seeded
1/4 cup wine vinegar
1 cup Spanish olive oil

Combine all ingredients except olive oil in blender container. Add 1/4 cup of the olive oil. Blend until smooth. Slowly add remaining olive oil while continuing to blend at high speed. Mixture will thicken. Serve with meat, seafood, or vegetables. Makes 6 servings.

To prepare without blender, use ground almonds and crushed garlic. Then prepare as above using an egg beater.

CALORIES PER SERVING 383
GRAMS OF PROTEIN PER SERVING 2
GRAMS OF CARBOHYDRATE PER SERVING 2
GRAMS OF FAT PER SERVING 41

Stir-Fry Zucchini

4 cups sliced zucchini (about 1/4-inch thick)
1/4 cup Spanish olive oil
1 to 2 teaspoons oregano
2 teaspoons sugar
1 teaspoon salt

Saute zucchini in skillet with olive oil and seasonings until tender, about 15 minutes, stirring frequently. Makes 6 servings.

CALORIES PER SERVING 113
GRAMS OF PROTEIN PER SERVING 1
GRAMS OF CARBOHYDRATE PER SERVING 6
GRAMS OF FAT PER SERVING 9

Cool Sour Cream Sauces

1 tablespoon Spanish olive oil
    Selected Seasoning (see below)
1 cup (1/2 pt.) sour cream

Heat olive oil with selected seasoning in small saucepan for several minutes. Remove from heat. Stir in sour cream. Chill until ready to use. Serve as sauce for hot or cold meat, seafood or vegetables; or as a topping for salads; or as a spread for sandwiches; or as a dip. Makes 1 cup.

Selected Seasonings:

1 teaspoon dill seeds. Serve over cooked fish, use as dip for shrimp, or a topping for sliced cucumbers.
1 teaspoon mustard seeds. A nice sauce for cooked cabbage.
1 teaspoon curry powder. Try this as a spread on roast beef or ham sandwiches.
1 teaspoon cumin seeds. Perfect with chicken or turkey. Also good over cooked green beans.
1 teaspoon grated lemon rind. Tasty with asparagus or poached fish.
1 clove garlic, crushed, and 1 tablespoon chopped chives. Interesting with pork and also with cauliflower or sliced tomatoes.

CALORIES PER SERVING 578
GRAMS OF PROTEIN PER SERVING 6
GRAMS OF CARBOHYDRATE PER SERVING 7
GRAMS OF FAT PER SERVING 57

Garlic Sauce

    1 medium potato, cooked
    2 cloves garlic, crushed
    1 cup Spanish olive oil
    2 tablespoons wine vinegar
 1/2 teaspoon salt
       Dash pepper

Mash potato; stir in garlic. Gradually beat in olive oil. Stir in vinegar, salt, and pepper. Serve over hamburgers, lamburgers, steaks or chops, or over vegetables. Makes 6 servings.

CALORIES PER SERVING 344
GRAMS OF PROTEIN PER SERVING 0
GRAMS OF CARBOHYDRATE PER SERVING 3
GRAMS OF FAT PER SERVING 37

Crunchy Seasoned Crumbs

    2 cups fresh bread crumbs
    2 tablespoons Spanish olive oil
    1 teaspoon paprika
 1/2 teaspoon salt
 1/8 teaspoon pepper

Saute crumbs in olive oil over low heat until golden, about 10 minutes, stirring often. Stir in seasonings. Cool to room temperature. Spoon over hot cooked vegetables, over scrambled or fried eggs, over sliced tomatoes or a tossed salad. Makes 32 servings.

CALORIES PER TABLESPOON 29
GRAMS OF PROTEIN PER TABLESPOON 0
GRAMS OF CARBOHYDRATE PER TABLESPOON 4
GRAMS OF FAT PER TABLESPOON 1

Italian Tomato Sauce

 1/4 cup Spanish olive oil
    1 cup chopped onion
    1 clove garlic
 1/2 cup minced parsley
    1 can (20 oz.) tomatoes with liquid
    1 can (6 oz.) tomato paste
    1 teaspoon sugar
 1/4 teaspoon salt
 1/8 teaspoon pepper

In skillet, heat olive oil with onion and garlic until tender, but not browned, about 3 minutes. Mash garlic; then add parsley, tomatoes, tomato paste, sugar, salt and pep-

per. Bring to a boil, reduce heat and simmer 45 minutes, stirring occasionally to break up pieces of tomato. Serve over spaghetti, cooked eggplant, meats or fish. Makes 12 servings.

CALORIES PER SERVING 71
GRAMS OF PROTEIN PER SERVING 1
GRAMS OF CARBOHYDRATE PER SERVING 6
GRAMS OF FAT PER SERVING 4

Raw Spinach Sauce

 1/2 pound spinach, coarsely chopped
    1 green pepper, chopped
    2 tablespoons chopped onion
 1/4 cup Spanish olive oil
 1/4 teaspoon salt
    1 teaspoon vinegar

Put chopped spinach and green pepper in electric blender, a handful at a time and mix at low speed. Add chopped onion; when fairly smooth, slowly add olive oil, salt and finally vinegar. Blend until of relish consistency (it will not be smooth). Serve over cooked vegetables. Makes about 6 servings.

CALORIES PER SERVING 97
GRAMS OF PROTEIN PER SERVING 1
GRAMS OF CARBOHYDRATE PER SERVING 2
GRAMS OF FAT PER SERVING 9

Granada Sauce

    1 medium tomato, peeled and chopped
    1 tablespoon chopped onion
 1/8 teaspoon ground cumin
    1 teaspoon crushed dried mint or 1
       tablespoon chopped fresh mint
    1 tablespoon Spanish olive oil
 1/4 cup sour cream
 1/4 teaspoon salt

Blend ingredients together with a fork or puree in blender. Serve at room temperature as sauce for vegetables, meat, or seafood. Makes 4 servings.

CALORIES PER SERVING 69
GRAMS OF PROTEIN PER SERVING 0
GRAMS OF CARBOHYDRATE PER SERVING 2
GRAMS OF FAT PER SERVING 6

Super-Smooth Sauce

    3 tablespoons Spanish olive oil
    3 tablespoons flour
 3/4 teaspoon salt
 1/2 teaspoon dry mustard
 3/4 cup milk
 3/4 cup half and half or light cream

In saucepan, mix olive oil, flour, salt and
mustard. Gradually stir in milk and cream.
Cook and stir over medium heat until thick
and smooth. Use as a sauce for vegetables,
add cut-up cooked meats, or follow any of
the variations below to make a completely
new sauce. Makes 6 servings.

```
CALORIES PER SERVING .............................. 136
GRAMS OF PROTEIN PER SERVING ................... 2
GRAMS OF CARBOHYDRATE PER SERVING ........... 5
GRAMS OF FAT PER SERVING ........................ 11
```

Tomato Sauce . . . Mix in 1 1/2 tablespoons
tomato paste or catsup.

Seasoned Sauce . . . Add 3/4 teaspoon of any
one of the following: garlic salt, onion salt
or paprika.

Green Sauce . . . Stir in 1/4 cup finely chopped parsley, fresh dill or green onion tops.

Cheese Sauce . . . Stir in 1/2 cup grated
cheese (Cheddar, Mozzarella, Blue, Swiss
or Muenster).

Oriental Sauce

    1 medium tomato, chopped
    1 small onion, sliced
 1/8 teaspoon cumin or curry powder
    1 teaspoon dried mint, or 3 or 4 sprigs of fresh
      mint, chopped
 1/2 teaspoon salt
 1/4 cup Spanish olive oil
    1 teaspoon vinegar

Combine tomato, onion, cumin, mint and
salt in blender container. Set blender at low
speed; slowly add olive oil and finally
vinegar. Serve over cooked vegetables.
Makes 4 servings.

```
CALORIES PER SERVING .............................. 142
GRAMS OF PROTEIN PER SERVING ................... 0
GRAMS OF CARBOHYDRATE PER SERVING ........... 4
GRAMS OF FAT PER SERVING ........................ 14
```

Pasta, Potatoes, Rice:

The nutrients in pasta, potatoes and rice are important for a balanced diet. If you're counting calories or carbohydrates, just watch the size of the serving . . . and use olive oil to create new, different taste treats.

Potato Salad with Shrimp

    1 envelope garlic salad dressing mix
 1/4 cup wine vinegar
    2 tablespoons water
 2/3 cup Spanish olive oil
    1 pound shelled shrimp, cooked
    6 cups diced, cooked potatoes (hot)
 1/3 cup finely chopped onion
 1/2 cup chopped parsley
    1 medium cucumber, peeled, and cut length-
        wise into 8 strips
    1 tomato, sliced
    1 avocado, peeled, cut into 8 strips
        Iceberg or Boston lettuce
    1 tablespoon capers

Prepare salad dressing mix with vinegar, water and olive oil as directed on envelope. Reserve 9 shrimp for garnish. Chop remaining shrimp. Combine potatoes, onion, chopped shrimp and parsley in bowl, and toss with 2/3 cup of the dressing. Marinate remaining shrimp, tomato slices, cucumber and avocado strips in remaining dressing. Line a large oval platter with the lettuce, and mound the potato salad in the center. Stand marinated shrimp and cucumber strips on end alternately around sides of mound. Sprinkle capers over top. Garnish with avocado and tomato slices arranged around base. Makes 6 servings.

CALORIES PER SERVING 415
GRAMS OF PROTEIN PER SERVING 18
GRAMS OF CARBOHYDRATE PER SERVING 26
GRAMS OF FAT PER SERVING 27

Home Fried Potatoes

    3 medium potatoes
    2 cups boiling, salted water
    2 tablespoons flour
    3 tablespoons Spanish olive oil
 1/2 cup minced onions
        Salt and pepper to taste

Cook potatoes in boiling salted water in a covered saucepan until just tender, about 25 minutes. Drain and cover with cold water. When cool enough to handle, peel and slice potatoes about 1/4 inch thick. Coat with flour. Put olive oil in 8-inch frying pan, and roll olive oil over bottom and sides of pan. Place about a third of the potatoes in a layer in the pan. Sprinkle with about half the onions and some salt and pepper. Add another layer of potatoes, the remaining onions and some salt and pepper. Top with remaining potatoes. Press down gently. Cook, uncovered, over moderate heat about 10 minutes or until bottom side is golden brown. Loosen with spatula and turn out onto a flat plate. Slide back into pan with browned side on top. Cook about another 8 minutes or until other side is golden brown. Makes 4 servings.

CALORIES PER SERVING 203
GRAMS OF PROTEIN PER SERVING 3
GRAMS OF CARBOHYDRATE PER SERVING 24
GRAMS OF FAT PER SERVING 10

Cheesed Potato Cakes

    2 cups grated raw potatoes
      Ice water
  1/2 cup chopped onion
    2 tablespoons Spanish olive oil
  1/4 cup grated Cheddar cheese
    1 egg, slightly beaten
  1/4 teaspoon salt
  1/8 teaspoon pepper
  1/4 cup Spanish olive oil

Place grated potatoes in ice water for a few minutes; then drain and pat dry. Saute onion in 2 tablespoons olive oil until tender, but not browned. Mix with potatoes, cheese, egg, salt and pepper. Heat remaining olive oil in skillet. Using a 1/4 cup measure, scoop up potato mixture and ease into skillet. When cakes have browned on one side, turn and brown other side. Three or four may be cooked at the same time. Add more oil as necessary. Makes 4 servings, of 2 cakes each.

```
CALORIES PER SERVING . . . . . . . . . . . . . . . . . . . . . . . . . . 317
GRAMS OF PROTEIN PER SERVING . . . . . . . . . . . . . . . . . 5
GRAMS OF CARBOHYDRATE PER SERVING . . . . . . . . . . . 18
GRAMS OF FAT PER SERVING . . . . . . . . . . . . . . . . . . . . . 24
```

Spanish Fried Potatoes

    3 tablespoons Spanish olive oil
    4 medium potatoes, sliced
    1 large onion, sliced
    1 clove garlic, crushed
  1/4 teaspoon saffron
  1/2 teaspoon salt
    6 blanched, slivered almonds

Heat olive oil in large heavy skillet. Add potatoes, onion, garlic, saffron, salt and almonds. Cook over low heat, turning occasionally, until potatoes are golden and tender, about 25 to 30 minutes. Makes 6 servings.

```
CALORIES PER SERVING . . . . . . . . . . . . . . . . . . . . . . . . . . 111
GRAMS OF PROTEIN PER SERVING . . . . . . . . . . . . . . . . . 1
GRAMS OF CARBOHYDRATE PER SERVING . . . . . . . . . . . 11
GRAMS OF FAT PER SERVING . . . . . . . . . . . . . . . . . . . . . 7
```

Spanish-Style Spaghetti

  1/4 cup Spanish olive oil
    1 cup chopped onion
    1 clove garlic
  1/2 cup minced parsley
    1 can (28 oz.) peeled tomatoes
    1 can (6 oz.) tomato paste
    1 teaspoon sugar
  1/4 teaspoon salt
  1/8 teaspoon pepper
    2 cups diced cooked turkey or chicken
    1 pound spaghetti, cooked and drained

In skillet, heat olive oil with onion and garlic and saute until tender, but not browned. Mash garlic; add parsley, tomatoes, tomato paste, sugar, salt and pepper. Bring to a boil, reduce heat, and simmer 45 minutes, stirring occasionally to break up pieces of tomato. Add turkey or chicken and simmer several minutes. Serve over spaghetti. Makes 8 servings.

```
CALORIES PER SERVING . . . . . . . . . . . . . . . . . . . . . . . . . . 430
GRAMS OF PROTEIN PER SERVING . . . . . . . . . . . . . . . . . 21
GRAMS OF CARBOHYDRATE PER SERVING . . . . . . . . . . . 52
GRAMS OF FAT PER SERVING . . . . . . . . . . . . . . . . . . . . . 14
```

Marinara

  1/2 cup Spanish olive oil
    2 cloves garlic, crushed
    2 cans (28 oz. *each*) Italian plum tomatoes, drained and crushed
  1/2 teaspoon basil
    6 anchovy fillets (optional)
    6 eggs
    1 pound spaghetti, cooked and drained
      Parsley

Heat olive oil in heavy pan and brown garlic. Add tomatoes, basil and anchovies and simmer 45 minutes. Slip one egg per person into sauce; cover pan and poach eggs until slightly firm. Pour sauce over cooked spaghetti. Garnish with poached egg and parsley. Makes 6 servings.

```
CALORIES PER SERVING . . . . . . . . . . . . . . . . . . . . . . . . . . 573
GRAMS OF PROTEIN PER SERVING . . . . . . . . . . . . . . . . . 18
GRAMS OF CARBOHYDRATE PER SERVING . . . . . . . . . . . 64
GRAMS OF FAT PER SERVING . . . . . . . . . . . . . . . . . . . . . 26
```

Spaghetti Al Pesto

 2 tablespoons salt
 4 to 6 quarts boiling water
 1 pound spaghetti
 2 cups firmly-packed Italian or curly edge
   parsley
 2 tablespoons fresh basil (or 1 teaspoon
   dried basil leaves)
 3 cloves garlic
 3/4 cup Spanish olive oil
 3 tablespoons butter
 1/2 cup freshly grated Romano cheese
 1/2 cup freshly grated Parmesan cheese
 1 1/2 teaspoons salt
 1/4 teaspoon pepper

Add 2 tablespoons salt to rapidly boiling water. Gradually add spaghetti so that water continues to boil. Cook uncovered, stirring occasionally until tender. Drain. Meanwhile, combine remaining ingredients in electric blender. Blend at high speed until mixture looks almost like a paste, but with some specks of parsley still visible. Add to spaghetti and toss until spaghetti is completely coated. Makes 8 servings.

CALORIES PER SERVING 555
GRAMS OF PROTEIN PER SERVING 17
GRAMS OF CARBOHYDRATE PER SERVING 46
GRAMS OF FAT PER SERVING 33

Lemon Clam Spaghetti

 1/2 cup butter
 3 tablespoons Spanish olive oil
 1/3 cup finely chopped onion
 2 cloves garlic, crushed
 2 cans (8 oz. *each*) minced clams, drained
   (save liquid)
 3 tablespoons lemon juice
 1 tablespoon chopped parsley
 2 teaspoons grated lemon peel
 1/4 teaspoon pepper
 1 bay leaf
 1 pound spaghetti, cooked and drained
 1 cup grated Parmesan cheese
 6 lemon wedges

Heat 3 tablespoons butter and olive oil in heavy pan. Saute onion and garlic until tender. Add liquid from clams, lemon juice, parsley, lemon peel, pepper and bay leaf; simmer until liquid is reduced to about 1 cup. Remove bay leaf. Stir in clams and heat thoroughly. Add remaining butter; stir until melted. Pour sauce over spaghetti, sprinkle with cheese and serve with lemon wedges. Makes 8 servings.

CALORIES PER SERVING 508
GRAMS OF PROTEIN PER SERVING 22
GRAMS OF CARBOHYDRATE PER SERVING 47
GRAMS OF FAT PER SERVING 24

Rice Pilaf

  2 tablespoons Spanish olive oil
  1 cup uncooked rice
1/2 cup chopped onion
3/4 teaspoon salt
1/8 teaspoon pepper
1/2 teaspoon oregano
1 3/4 cups water
  2 beef bouillon cubes
  1 tablespoon Spanish olive oil
1/3 cup slivered blanched almonds
  1 tablespoon chopped parsley

Heat 2 tablespoons olive oil in a 2-quart saucepan. Add rice. Stir constantly until rice is golden brown. Add onion, salt, pepper, oregano, water and bouillon cubes. When cubes are dissolved, cover and simmer over low heat 20 minutes or until rice is tender and liquid is absorbed. Heat 1 tablespoon olive oil in a small saucepan. Stir in almonds and saute until lightly browned. Stir almonds and parsley into rice. Makes 6 servings.

CALORIES PER SERVING 159
GRAMS OF PROTEIN PER SERVING 2
GRAMS OF CARBOHYDRATE PER SERVING 18
GRAMS OF FAT PER SERVING 8

Rice a la Riojana

1 onion, sliced
2 tablespoons Spanish olive oil
1 cup uncooked rice
3 cups water
3 chicken bouillon cubes
1 tablespoon minced parsley
1 small jar (4 oz.) pimientoes, drained and cut in large pieces

Saute onion in olive oil until tender. Add rice and stir to coat thoroughly with the olive oil. Add water and bouillon cubes, minced parsley and red peppers. Cook uncovered until all liquid is absorbed and rice is fluffy; this may take about 1 hour. Cover during last 10 or 15 minutes to make sure all rice is soft. Serve with Spanish Mayonnaise as a sauce. Makes 6 servings.

CALORIES PER SERVING 136
GRAMS OF PROTEIN PER SERVING 2
GRAMS OF CARBOHYDRATE PER SERVING 20
GRAMS OF FAT PER SERVING 4

Elegant Saffron Rice

  1 pinch of saffron threads
  2 tablespoons water
1/3 cup chopped scallions (or onion)
  2 tablespoons Spanish olive oil
  2 cups chicken broth
  1 cup uncooked rice
  3 strips lemon peel
  1 clove garlic, crushed
  1 teaspoon salt
1/4 teaspoon oregano
1/8 teaspoon dried thyme
1/8 teaspoon freshly ground pepper
1/3 cup toasted, slivered blanched almonds
1/4 cup diced pimiento
1/2 cup coarsely chopped olives

Combine saffron and water; let saffron steep in water 5 minutes. Meanwhile, saute scallions in olive oil until tender. Then stir in chicken broth, rice, lemon peel, garlic and seasonings. Bring to boil, stir; reduce heat, cover and simmer 15 minutes (or until rice is tender and liquid is absorbed). Fluff with fork. Remove lemon peel. Stir in remaining ingredients. Cover and heat 1 minute before serving. Makes 6 servings.

CALORIES PER SERVING 162
GRAMS OF PROTEIN PER SERVING 3
GRAMS OF CARBOHYDRATE PER SERVING 19
GRAMS OF FAT PER SERVING 7

Rice Parmesan

6 cups cooked rice, cooked in chicken broth
2 cans (4 oz. *each*) sliced mushrooms, drained
2 cups cooked green peas
2 tablespoons Spanish olive oil
2 tablespoons butter
  Salt and pepper to taste
1/2 cup grated Parmesan cheese
6 tablespoons chopped parsley

Combine hot rice, mushrooms, peas, olive oil, butter, and seasonings. Heat until vegetables are hot, about 3 or 4 minutes. Add Parmesan cheese and toss lightly. Turn into serving bowl and garnish with chopped parsley. Makes 12 servings.

CALORIES PER SERVING 152
GRAMS OF PROTEIN PER SERVING 4
GRAMS OF CARBOHYDRATE PER SERVING 20
GRAMS OF FAT PER SERVING 5

Salads:
The golden smoothness of Spanish olive oil complements practically all salad ingredients. And its unique ability to blend without cooking makes olive oil the "Star" performer here.

Spanish Salad, American Style

  2 **large oranges, peeled, sliced, and cut in half**
  1 **small onion, thinly sliced**
  2 **tomatoes, sliced and quartered**
 10 **cooked asparagus spears (halved)**
1/2 **cup Spanish olive oil**
1/4 **teaspoon salt**
1/4 **cup vinegar**
  1 **ripe avocado, sliced**
  6 to 8 **radishes**
  8 **pimiento-stuffed olives**
    Salad greens

Place orange and onion slices, tomato and asparagus in a bowl with olive oil, salt and vinegar. Marinate 1/2 hour. Add avocado, radishes, olives. Arrange on salad greens and serve immediately. Makes 6 servings.

```
CALORIES PER SERVING ............................ 232
GRAMS OF PROTEIN PER SERVING ................... 2
GRAMS OF CARBOHYDRATE PER SERVING ........... 7
GRAMS OF FAT PER SERVING ....................... 22
```

Marinated Tomato Salad

  3 **medium tomatoes, sliced**
  3 **small onions, thinly sliced**
1/2 **cup Oil and Vinegar Dressing**
  2 **tablespoons chopped parsley**

Combine tomato and onion slices. Add dressing and chill at least 2 hours. Sprinkle with parsley. Makes 4 servings.

```
CALORIES PER SERVING ............................ 244
GRAMS OF PROTEIN PER SERVING ................... 2
GRAMS OF CARBOHYDRATE PER SERVING ........... 13
GRAMS OF FAT PER SERVING ....................... 21
```

Mandarin Chicken Salad

  2 **cups cooked cubed chicken**
  1 **tablespoon minced onion**
  1 **teaspoon salt**
  1 **cup seedless grapes, halved**
  1 **cup diced celery**
  1 **can (11 oz.) mandarin orange segments, drained**
  1 **cup Spanish mayonnaise**
1/3 **cup slivered almonds**
  1 **tablespoon lemon juice**
1/2 **teaspoon grated lemon peel (optional)**
  1 **cup (4 oz.) macaroni rings or elbow macaroni, cooked and drained**
  1 **cup whipping cream**

Combine chicken, onion and salt; refrigerate several hours. Add grapes, celery, orange segments, mayonnaise, almonds, lemon juice and peel to chicken mixture. Stir cooked pasta into chicken mixture. When ready to serve, whip cream and fold into chicken mixture. Serve on lettuce leaves. Makes 8 servings.

```
CALORIES PER SERVING ............................ 500
GRAMS OF PROTEIN PER SERVING ................... 11
GRAMS OF CARBOHYDRATE PER SERVING ........... 23
GRAMS OF FAT PER SERVING ....................... 40
```

Spanish Chicken Salad

3½ cups diced cooked chicken*
  1 large onion, thinly sliced
  1 small crisp head lettuce, shredded
  3 medium tomatoes, cut in wedges
½ cup Spanish olive oil
¼ cup red wine vinegar
  1 teaspoon salt
½ teaspoon black pepper
  2 oranges, peeled and sliced
  2 avocados, sliced
  1 bunch small radishes, trimmed

Toss together chicken, onion slices, lettuce and tomatoes with dressing of olive oil, vinegar, salt and pepper. Arrange on lettuce leaves; garnish with orange and avocado slices and small whole radishes. Makes 8 luncheon servings.

*Note: One 3-pound chicken, cooked, will make this amount cooked chicken, or use three 12-ounce cans pure chicken meat. Leftover cooked turkey, diced, may also be used.

CALORIES PER SERVING 300
GRAMS OF PROTEIN PER SERVING 9
GRAMS OF CARBOHYDRATE PER SERVING 9
GRAMS OF FAT PER SERVING 26

Queen's Caprice Salad

4 to 6 Belgian endives
1 large tart apple, cored, unpeeled, cut in thin slices
½ cup diced celery
4 large fresh mushrooms, thinly sliced
1 tablespoon Spanish olive oil
1 teaspoon lemon juice
¼ teaspoon salt
1 medium can grapefruit sections, drained
   Spanish olive oil and salt
   Watercress
½ cup mayonnaise

Separate leaves of the endives, soak in ice-cold water, pat dry, then chill in vegetable freshener. Combine apple slices, celery and mushrooms, toss with the olive oil, lemon juice and salt and let stand half an hour before serving. Pile this mixture in center of endive; arrange grapefruit sections around it. Sprinkle grapefruit sections with olive oil and salt. Garnish with watercress. Serve with mayonnaise. Makes 4 servings.

CALORIES PER SERVING 338
GRAMS OF PROTEIN PER SERVING 2
GRAMS OF CARBOHYDRATE PER SERVING 17
GRAMS OF FAT PER SERVING 29

Spanish Citrus Salad

¼ cup Spanish olive oil
3 tablespoons frozen grapefruit juice concentrate, thawed
1 tablespoon vinegar
1 cup chopped celery
1 tablespoon onion, minced
1 tablespoon minced parsley
1 tablespoon minced pimiento
1 teaspoon salt
¼ teaspoon oregano
   Pinch thyme
1 can (17 oz.) kidney beans, drained
2 oranges, separated into sections

Combine all ingredients. Toss to blend. Let marinate about 2 hours before serving. Makes 6 servings.

CALORIES PER SERVING 220
GRAMS OF PROTEIN PER SERVING 7
GRAMS OF CARBOHYDRATE PER SERVING 27
GRAMS OF FAT PER SERVING 9

Curried Avocado and Tangerine Salad

1/2 teaspoon curry powder
1/2 teaspoon salt
1/2 tablespoon lemon juice
 3 tablespoons Spanish olive oil
 2 ripe avocados
 2 tangerines
   Large bunch watercress

For the dressing, mix curry powder and salt. Slowly add lemon juice, then olive oil. Peel and slice avocados; marinate in the dressing until time to serve, making sure slices are completely covered with dressing to prevent discoloring. Peel tangerines, divide each into sections and carefully remove all white membrane. Combine these with the marinated avocados and serve over watercress. Makes 4 servings.

```
CALORIES PER SERVING . . . . . . . . . . . . . . . . . . . . . . . . . . . . 284
GRAMS OF PROTEIN PER SERVING . . . . . . . . . . . . . . . . . . .   2
GRAMS OF CARBOHYDRATE PER SERVING . . . . . . . . . . .  12
GRAMS OF FAT PER SERVING . . . . . . . . . . . . . . . . . . . . . . .  26
```

Caesar Salad

 1 clove garlic
 2 heads romaine or other lettuce
1/4 teaspoon dry mustard
   Salt and pepper to taste
 3 ounces (1/2 of a 6-oz. package)
   Swiss cheese, finely diced
 4 anchovies, diced
1/2 cup Spanish olive oil
1/4 cup lemon juice
 1 cup croutons
 2 eggs
 1 slice Swiss cheese, finely diced

Rub salad bowl with garlic. Remove. Add romaine torn into bite-sized pieces, seasonings, diced cheese, anchovies, half of the olive oil and the lemon juice. Toss gently but thoroughly. Pour remainder of oil over croutons and toss well. Break eggs over salad and mix gently until well blended. Add croutons and toss again. Garnish with remaining cheese. Makes 6 servings.

```
CALORIES PER SERVING . . . . . . . . . . . . . . . . . . . . . . . . . . . . 415
GRAMS OF PROTEIN PER SERVING . . . . . . . . . . . . . . . . . . .  13
GRAMS OF CARBOHYDRATE PER SERVING . . . . . . . . . . .  29
GRAMS OF FAT PER SERVING . . . . . . . . . . . . . . . . . . . . . . .  27
```

Hot Pork Sliver Salad

 1 head iceberg lettuce
 1 can (29 oz.) pear halves
 2 large pork chops (about 1 lb.)
1/3 cup vinegar
 3 tablespoons soy sauce
 2 teaspoons dry mustard
 2 teaspoons seasoned salt
 1 teaspoon sugar
1/4 teaspoon white pepper
1/4 cup Spanish olive oil

Core, rinse and thoroughly drain lettuce; chill in plastic bag or plastic crisper. When crisp, tear bite-size pieces to yield 5 cups. Drain pears and cut each half lengthwise into two pieces. Gently toss lettuce and pears together in large salad bowl. Cut pork off bones and thinly slice to yield 1 1/2 cups. Combine vinegar, soy sauce, mustard salt, sugar and pepper. Heat olive oil in skillet until sizzling hot. Add pork and cook, stirring, 1 to 2 minutes or until done. Add vinegar mixture; heat 1 minute longer. Pour hot sauce over the lettuce mixture and toss well to coat. Serve at once. Makes 4 luncheon servings.

```
CALORIES PER SERVING . . . . . . . . . . . . . . . . . . . . . . . . . . . . 570
GRAMS OF PROTEIN PER SERVING . . . . . . . . . . . . . . . . . . .  15
GRAMS OF CARBOHYDRATE PER SERVING . . . . . . . . . . .  47
GRAMS OF FAT PER SERVING . . . . . . . . . . . . . . . . . . . . . . .  36
```

Ham and Cheese Salad

 2 cups diced cooked ham
1/4 pound (3/4 c.) American cheese, cut into thin
   strips
1/2 cup cooked or canned peas
1/2 cup chopped celery
 1 head lettuce, broken into bite-size pieces
1/4 cup India, cucumber or sweet relish
 2 tablespoons salad or cider vinegar
1/4 cup Spanish olive oil
 1 teaspoon salt
   Dash pepper

Lightly toss ingredients together. Chill about 1/2 hour. Makes 8 servings.

```
CALORIES PER SERVING . . . . . . . . . . . . . . . . . . . . . . . . . . . . 158
GRAMS OF PROTEIN PER SERVING . . . . . . . . . . . . . . . . . . .   7
GRAMS OF CARBOHYDRATE PER SERVING . . . . . . . . . . .   2
GRAMS OF FAT PER SERVING . . . . . . . . . . . . . . . . . . . . . . .  12
```

Western Mushroom Salad

    1 head iceberg lettuce
    1/4 pound fresh mushrooms
    1/3 cup clam juice
    1/3 cup Spanish olive oil
    2 tablespoons vinegar
    1/4 to 1/2 teaspoon salt
    1/4 teaspoon tarragon, crumbled
        Tabasco sauce to taste
    1 cup sliced red onion
    1 tomato

Core, rinse and thoroughly drain lettuce. Refrigerate in plastic bag or plastic crisper. Rinse and scrub mushrooms; cut off dry tips of stems. Slice mushrooms lengthwise. Combine clam juice, olive oil, vinegar, salt, tarragon and Tabasco in large jar; cover and shake well. Add mushrooms and onion; shake to coat. Chill. Tear enough lettuce to make 5 cups; chill remainder for use another time. Cut tomato into wedges and combine with rest of salad in large salad bowl; toss lightly. Makes 6 servings.

CALORIES PER SERVING 131
GRAMS OF PROTEIN PER SERVING 1
GRAMS OF CARBOHYDRATE PER SERVING 4
GRAMS OF FAT PER SERVING 12

Iceberg Wedges a la Pimiento

    1 head iceberg lettuce
    1 can (7 oz.) whole pimientos
    3 tablespoons Spanish olive oil
    4 teaspoons lemon juice
    1/4 teaspoon salt
    1/8 teaspoon pepper
        Few drops Tabasco sauce
    2 tablespoons sliced green onion

Core, rinse and thoroughly drain lettuce; refrigerate in plastic bag or plastic crisper. Puree pimientos in blender; mix with all remaining ingredients except lettuce. Cut lettuce into 6 wedges; place on salad plates. Spoon pimiento dressing over wedges. Makes 6 servings.

CALORIES PER SERVING 83
GRAMS OF PROTEIN PER SERVING 1
GRAMS OF CARBOHYDRATE PER SERVING 4
GRAMS OF FAT PER SERVING 7

Rice and Salmon Salad

    3 cups cooked rice
    1 cup grated American cheese
    1 cup cleaned, flaked salmon
    1 cup chopped walnuts
    1 cup chopped celery
    1/4 cup cider vinegar
    3/4 cup Spanish olive oil
    1/4 teaspoon paprika
    1/2 teaspoon salt
    1/2 teaspoon curry powder (or cumin)
    1 teaspoon sugar (optional)
        Lettuce leaves
    2 tomatoes, cut in wedges

Combine rice, cheese, salmon, walnuts and celery. Mix vinegar, olive oil, paprika, salt, curry and sugar in jar; shake well. Pour over rice mixture; toss lightly. Cover and chill. Serve on lettuce leaves and garnish with tomato wedges or use as a stuffing for tomatoes. Makes 6 servings.

CALORIES PER SERVING 727
GRAMS OF PROTEIN PER SERVING 20
GRAMS OF CARBOHYDRATE PER SERVING 27
GRAMS OF FAT PER SERVING 61

Pear Frijole Salad

    1 can (29 oz.) pear halves
    1/3 cup pear syrup
    1/3 cup Spanish olive oil
    1/4 cup vinegar
    2 drops Tabasco sauce
    1 clove garlic, minced
    1/4 teaspoon salt
    1 can (16 oz.) kidney beans, drained
    3/4 cup sliced celery
    1 small onion, sliced
        Crisp lettuce

Drain pears, reserving 1/3 cup syrup. Combine pear syrup, olive oil, vinegar, Tabasco, garlic and salt. Pour over pears. Marinate in refrigerator 1/2 hour. Combine kidney beans, celery, and onion slices, separated into rings. Arrange pear halves and bean mixture on lettuce-lined plates. Drizzle with marinade. Makes 6 servings.

CALORIES PER SERVING 322
GRAMS OF PROTEIN PER SERVING 6
GRAMS OF CARBOHYDRATE PER SERVING 47
GRAMS OF FAT PER SERVING 13

Lasagne Caesar Salad

1/2 cup Spanish olive oil
2 1/2 tablespoons white vinegar
1 clove garlic, minced
1 teaspoon salt
1/2 teaspoon sugar
1/2 teaspoon anchovy paste
1/4 teaspoon pepper
1/8 teaspoon dry mustard
1/2 pound (8 oz.) lasagne noodles, cooked
1 egg yolk
1 large head romaine lettuce
2 cups garlic-flavored croutons
1/4 cup grated Parmesan cheese

Combine olive oil, vinegar, garlic, salt, sugar, anchovy paste, pepper and dry mustard. Cut lasagne noodles into 1/4″ x 2″ strips; place in large bowl. Add egg yolk and toss to mix; add olive oil dressing and toss. Tear romaine into small chunks and add to noodle mixture. Add half of the croutons and half of the cheese; toss to mix. Garnish with remaining croutons and cheese. Makes 6 servings.

```
CALORIES PER SERVING ............................. 591
GRAMS OF PROTEIN PER SERVING .................. 16
GRAMS OF CARBOHYDRATE PER SERVING ........... 76
GRAMS OF FAT PER SERVING ....................... 25
```

Lettuce Fruit Silos

1 head iceberg lettuce
2 envelopes plain gelatin
1/2 cup cold water
1 teaspoon prepared mustard
1/2 cup sugar
1/4 teaspoon salt
2 cups boiling water
1/2 cup lemon juice
Few drops Tabasco sauce
1 can (16 oz.) cling peach slices
Radish slices

Core, rinse and drain lettuce well. Remove 6 to 8 outer leaves. Cut remaining lettuce lengthwise into halves; place cut-sides down on chopping board. Shred across heart with sharp knife to make 1 cup. Place remainder and outer leaves in plastic bag or plastic crisper; chill. Soften gelatin in cold water; stir in mustard, sugar and salt. Add boiling

water; stir until gelatin and sugar are completely dissolved. Stir in lemon juice and Tabasco. Set aside 1 1/2 cups gelatin mixture. Chill remaining mixture until it mounds on spoon; fold in shredded lettuce. Turn into 6 to 8 individual molds; chill to a soft set. Meanwhile, drain peaches well. Chill reserved gelatin until it mounds on spoon; fold in peaches. Turn into molds over lettuce layer. Chill until firm. Unmold on bed made of lettuce leaves. Garnish with radish slices. Makes 6 servings.

```
CALORIES PER SERVING ............................. 111
GRAMS OF PROTEIN PER SERVING .................... 4
GRAMS OF CARBOHYDRATE PER SERVING ........... 24
GRAMS OF FAT PER SERVING ........................ 0
```

Avocado Tossed Salad

1 head iceberg lettuce
1/2 cup Spanish olive oil
1 clove garlic, peeled
2 tablespoons wine vinegar
1/2 teaspoon salt
Freshly ground black pepper
1/4 teaspoon paprika
1/2 teaspoon aromatic bitters
1 red onion, sliced
1 avocado

Core, rinse and thoroughly drain lettuce; chill in lettuce crisper or plastic bag. Combine olive oil, garlic, vinegar, salt, pepper, paprika and bitters; let stand 1 hour. Discard garlic. Save outer lettuce leaves to line bowl and tear remainder into bite-size pieces. Break onion into rings over top. Peel and remove seed from avocado; slice in crescents; add to salad. Stir dressing; pour over salad and toss lightly to coat well. Line salad bowl with outer lettuce leaves, and tumble salad mixture into center. Makes 4 servings.

```
CALORIES PER SERVING ............................. 358
GRAMS OF PROTEIN PER SERVING .................... 2
GRAMS OF CARBOHYDRATE PER SERVING ............ 8
GRAMS OF FAT PER SERVING ....................... 36
```

*Vinagreta Sauce

  3 slices onion
  1 tablespoon minced parsley
1/2 teaspoon salt
  1 cup Spanish olive oil
  1 clove garlic, crushed
1/3 cup wine vinegar

Combine onion, parsley, salt, olive oil and garlic; let stand 1/2 hour. Remove garlic and discard; add vinegar, stir well. Makes 1 1/3 cups.

```
CALORIES PER SERVING .............................. 517
GRAMS OF PROTEIN PER SERVING ................... 11
GRAMS OF CARBOHYDRATE PER SERVING ........... 21
GRAMS OF FAT PER SERVING ....................... 44
```

King Crab Caesar Salad

  1 can (7 1/2 oz.) crab or 1 package (6 oz.)
       frozen crab
  1 clove garlic, peeled and quartered
1/3 cup Spanish olive oil
  2 quarts torn romaine lettuce (about 1 large
       head)
  1 small onion, thinly sliced
1/2 teaspoon salt
       Dash of freshly ground pepper
  1 teaspoon Worcestershire sauce
  1 egg, cooked in boiling water for 1 minute
  2 tablespoons lemon juice
1/3 cup grated Parmesan cheese
1 1/2 cups garlic-flavored croutons

Drain and slice canned crab, or defrost and slice frozen crab, set aside. Add garlic to oil and let stand for at least 1 hour. Remove garlic. Combine torn bite-size pieces of romaine with onion slices separated into rings. Toss with olive oil and sprinkle with salt, pepper and Worcestershire sauce. Break egg into salad. Add lemon juice and toss to mix. Add cheese, croutons and crab. Toss again. Serve immediately. Makes 6 servings.

```
CALORIES PER SERVING .............................. 378
GRAMS OF PROTEIN PER SERVING ................... 16
GRAMS OF CARBOHYDRATE PER SERVING ........... 39
GRAMS OF FAT PER SERVING ....................... 17
```

Hearty Chef Salad

  3 cups cooked rice
1/2 green pepper, diced
  1 pimiento, diced
  1 cup finely diced, cooked veal, turkey, or
       any leftover meat
1 1/3 cups Vinagreta Sauce*
  1 bottle (10 oz.) Spanish olives, drained
  1 medium tomato cut into wedges
  3 hard-cooked eggs

Combine rice with green pepper, pimiento and meat. Toss with 1/3 cup of the Vinagreta Sauce. Marinate olives and tomatoes in remaining sauce. Arrange rice mixture in a mound on platter with olives, tomatoes and egg wedges around the base. Serve chilled with remainder of sauce (left from marinating) and crisp French bread. Makes 6 servings.

West Coast Salad with Mushroom Dressing

        1 head iceberg lettuce
    1/4 cup wine vinegar
    1/2 cup Spanish olive oil
    1 1/2 teaspoons salt
        1 teaspoon paprika
            Freshly ground black pepper
        1 small clove garlic, crushed
    1/2 pound fresh mushrooms, sliced
    1/2 pound cooked, cleaned shrimp
        1 cup cooked or canned lobster or crab meat
        1 cup sliced celery
        1 package (10 oz.) frozen asparagus, cooked
        1 package (10 oz.) frozen peas, cooked
        2 hard-cooked eggs, sliced
        2 tomatoes, cut in wedges

Core, rinse and drain lettuce thoroughly; chill in disposable plastic bag or lettuce crisper. Combine vinegar, olive oil, salt, paprika, pepper and garlic in bowl; mix well. Add mushrooms, chill 1 hour. Half an hour before serving, separate lettuce leaves and line salad bowl; shred remaining lettuce into bottom of bowl. Arrange shrimp, lobster, celery, drained asparagus and peas in rows over lettuce. Spoon mushrooms onto salad. Stir the dressing and pour over salad. Garnish with egg slices and tomato wedges. Chill. Toss lightly before serving. Makes 8 servings.

```
CALORIES PER SERVING ............................. 249
GRAMS OF PROTEIN PER SERVING .................... 15
GRAMS OF CARBOHYDRATE PER SERVING ........... 11
GRAMS OF FAT PER SERVING ....................... 16
```

Spanish Orange and Onion Salad

            Salad greens
        2 oranges, peeled and sliced
        2 medium onions, thinly sliced
        1 small green pepper, slivered
        2 pimientos, drained and chopped
            White Wine Salad Dressing*

Line shallow bowl with greens. Arrange orange slices, onion rings, green pepper strips and chopped pimiento in an attractive pattern on the salad greens. Chill. Just before serving, drizzle with white wine salad dressing. Makes 4 servings.

*White Wine Salad Dressing

    3/4 cup dry white wine
    1/2 cup Spanish olive oil
    1/4 cup tarragon vinegar
    1/4 cup chopped onion
    1/2 clove garlic, minced
            Salt, pepper

Combine and blend ingredients.

```
CALORIES PER SERVING ............................. 388
GRAMS OF PROTEIN PER SERVING .................... 2
GRAMS OF CARBOHYDRATE PER SERVING ........... 19
GRAMS OF FAT PER SERVING ....................... 28
```

Chinese Banana and Seafood Salad

Mustard Dressing:

        2 tablespoons Spanish olive oil
        1 tablespoon prepared mustard
        1 tablespoon white wine or cider vinegar
        1 tablespoon lemon juice
    1/2 teaspoon salt
    1/2 teaspoon mustard seed
    1/4 teaspoon pepper

Measure all ingredients into a large bowl. Stir until well blended and smooth.

Salad:

    1 can (16. oz.) bean sprouts
    1 pound cooked and cleaned shrimp or 2 cans (6 1/2 or 7 oz. each) tuna
    1 can (8 3/4 oz.) pineapple tidbits, drained
    2 bananas

Drain bean sprouts, rinse in cold water, and drain again. Add to mustard dressing with shrimp and pineapple; mix well and chill. At serving time, peel bananas, cut into slices, and mix lightly with salad. Makes 4 servings.

```
CALORIES PER SERVING ............................. 319
GRAMS OF PROTEIN PER SERVING .................... 26
GRAMS OF CARBOHYDRATE PER SERVING ........... 38
GRAMS OF FAT PER SERVING ....................... 8
```

Salad Dressings:

Olive oil and salad dressings are almost synonomous! The dressings can vary . . . sweet or tangy, creamy or clear, thick or thin. Each adds new flavor, new character to the salad . . . to the meal.

Spanish Mayonnaise

2 egg yolks or 1 whole egg
1/2 teaspoon dry mustard
1/2 teaspoon salt
2 tablespoons vinegar, wine vinegar or lemon juice
1 cup Spanish olive oil

In a blender container, combine egg yolks, dry mustard, salt, vinegar and 1/4 cup of the olive oil. Cover; turn to high speed. Turn off, remove cover. Again turn blender to high and add remaining oil in a steady stream. Turn off. Refrigerate in a covered container until ready to use. Use as dressing for salads, or a dip for shrimp and vegetables. Makes 1 1/2 cups.

Easy Variations:

Red Mayonnaise: Add 1 teaspoon chili powder and paprika before blending.

Green Mayonnaise: Add 1/4 cup fresh basil or parsley before blending.

Zippy Blue Cheese Mayonnaise: After blending, stir in a 4-ounce package of crumbled blue cheese and 2 teaspoons aromatic bitters.

CALORIES PER TABLESPOON 86
GRAMS OF PROTEIN PER TABLESPOON 0
GRAMS OF CARBOHYDRATE PER TABLESPOON 0
GRAMS OF FAT PER TABLESPOON 9

French Dressing (American Version)

1 cup Spanish olive oil
1/4 cup vinegar
1/4 cup lemon juice
1 teaspoon salt
1/2 teaspoon dry mustard
1/2 teaspoon paprika

Combine all ingredients in a blender container and blend at high speed, or shake well in tightly covered jar. Store in covered jar in refrigerator. Allow to come to room temperature; then shake well before using. Makes 1 1/2 cups.

CALORIES PER TABLESPOON 83
GRAMS OF PROTEIN PER TABLESPOON 0
GRAMS OF CARBOHYDRATE PER TABLESPOON 0
GRAMS OF FAT PER TABLESPOON 9

Limeade or Lemonade Dressing

1/3 cup undiluted frozen concentrate for limeade or lemonade
1/3 cup honey
1/3 cup Spanish olive oil
1 teaspoon celery or poppy seeds

Combine all ingredients in a blender container and blend at high speed or in a small bowl and beat until smooth. Serve over fruit salads. Makes 1 cup.

CALORIES PER TABLESPOON 72
GRAMS OF PROTEIN PER TABLESPOON 0
GRAMS OF CARBOHYDRATE PER TABLESPOON 8
GRAMS OF FAT PER TABLESPOON 4

Vegetable Salad Dressing

    1 carrot, cut in pieces
    1 onion, quartered
    1 stalk celery, cut in pieces
    1 clove garlic
    1 teaspoon salt
 1/4 teaspoon pepper
    2 tablespoons vinegar
    1 egg
    1 cup Spanish olive oil

Place all ingredients except olive oil in blender and cover. Turn blender on and off rapidly until vegetables are pureed. Turn speed to high and gradually add olive oil in a thin stream, pausing now and then to allow mixture to thicken. Transfer to storage container, cover, and refrigerate overnight to allow flavors to blend. Spoon over salads when ready to serve. Makes 2 cups.

CALORIES PER TABLESPOON 67
GRAMS OF PROTEIN PER TABLESPOON 0
GRAMS OF CARBOHYDRATE PER TABLESPOON 0
GRAMS OF FAT PER TABLESPOON 7

Luncheon Salad Dressing

    1 cup mayonnaise
 1/4 cup vinegar
 1/2 cup Spanish olive oil
    1 tablespoon freeze-dried chives
    1 tablespoon seasoned salt
    3 hard-cooked eggs, finely chopped
    2 tablespoons finely chopped sweet pickle
    1 tablespoon finely chopped pimiento
    1 tablespoon Worcestershire sauce

Put mayonnaise in a bowl; add vinegar and olive oil alternately, a small amount at a time, beating well after each addition. Stir in remaining ingredients. Store in refrigerator in a covered container. Especially good with tomato or tossed green salads. Makes about 2 cups.

CALORIES PER TABLESPOON 91
GRAMS OF PROTEIN PER TABLESPOON 0
GRAMS OF CARBOHYDRATE PER TABLESPOON 0
GRAMS OF FAT PER TABLESPOON 9

Oil and Vinegar Dressing

 2/3 cup Spanish olive oil
 1/3 cup vinegar
    1 teaspoon sugar
    1 teaspoon salt
 1/4 teaspoon pepper

Combine ingredients in a covered jar. Shake to blend. Store at room temperature. Makes 1 cup dressing.

Easy Variations:

Garlic Dressing: Add 1 clove garlic to dressing. Let stand several hours or overnight. Remove the garlic before serving.

Dill Dressing: Add 1 teaspoon dill weed to dressing before serving.

Savory Dressing: Add a dash of Worcestershire sauce or soy sauce.

Honey Dressing: Substitute 1 tablespoon honey for the sugar.

CALORIES PER TABLESPOON 94
GRAMS OF PROTEIN PER TABLESPOON 0
GRAMS OF CARBOHYDRATE PER TABLESPOON 0
GRAMS OF FAT PER TABLESPOON 10

Oriental Salad Dressing

 1/4 teaspoon sugar
 1/4 teaspoon dry mustard
 1/4 teaspoon garlic powder
 1/4 teaspoon ginger
    1 tablespoon soy sauce
 1/2 cup Spanish olive oil
    2 tablespoons white wine vinegar
       Salt to taste

Combine all ingredients in a blender container and blend at high speed, or shake well in a covered jar. Good over vegetable and seafood salads. Makes 2/3 cup.

CALORIES PER TABLESPOON 94
GRAMS OF PROTEIN PER TABLESPOON 0
GRAMS OF CARBOHYDRATE PER TABLESPOON 0
GRAMS OF FAT PER TABLESPOON 10

Zesty Salad Dressing

1/2 tablespoon anchovy paste
1/2 teaspoon prepared mustard
3 tablespoons Spanish olive oil
1 tablespoon grated Parmesan cheese
1 tablespoon vinegar

Beat together anchovy paste and prepared mustard. Slowly beat in olive oil, Parmesan cheese and vinegar. Excellent with hard-boiled eggs and chicory. Makes about 1/3 cup.

```
CALORIES PER TABLESPOON .......................... 81
GRAMS OF PROTEIN PER TABLESPOON ............... 0
GRAMS OF CARBOHYDRATE PER TABLESPOON ........ 0
GRAMS OF FAT PER TABLESPOON ..................... 8
```

Onion French Dressing

1 cup Spanish olive oil
1/4 cup vinegar
1/4 cup lemon juice
1/2 teaspoon paprika
1/2 teaspoon dry mustard
1 teaspoon salt
2 tablespoons sugar
1 teaspoon onion juice

Combine all ingredients in pint jar or blender container. Cover and shake well or blend at high speed. Makes 1 1/2 cups.

```
CALORIES PER TABLESPOON .......................... 87
GRAMS OF PROTEIN PER TABLESPOON ............... 0
GRAMS OF CARBOHYDRATE PER TABLESPOON ........ 1
GRAMS OF FAT PER TABLESPOON ..................... 9
```

Apple Sauce Salad Dressing

1/2 cup Spanish olive oil
2 large (or 4 small) cloves garlic, quartered
1 medium onion, thinly sliced
1/2 cup apple sauce
1/4 cup vinegar
1 teaspoon salt
1/8 teaspoon pepper

Combine olive oil with garlic and onion. Let stand at room temperature for 2 to 3 hours. Remove garlic and onion. Stir in remaining ingredients. Store in refrigerator; allow to come to room temperature before using. Good on fruit salads, tossed salads or as a marinade for cooked vegetable salads. Makes 1 1/4 cups.

```
CALORIES PER TABLESPOON .......................... 57
GRAMS OF PROTEIN PER TABLESPOON ............... 0
GRAMS OF CARBOHYDRATE PER TABLESPOON ........ 2
GRAMS OF FAT PER TABLESPOON ..................... 5
```

Desserts:
A touch of sweetness to end the meal . . . and a final touch of Spanish olive oil! Recipes take on a smooth, moist texture. Oil adds a flavor accent without overpowering the sweetness of the other ingredients.

Christmas Fruit Cake

1/2 pound candied pineapple
1/2 pound candied citron
1/2 pound candied cherries
  3 cups seedless raisins
1 1/2 cups currants
1/2 cup apple juice
  3 cups sifted all-purpose flour
  1 teaspoon double-acting baking powder
  1 teaspoon salt
  2 teaspoons cinnamon
1/2 teaspoon nutmeg
1/4 teaspoon allspice
  1 cup Spanish olive oil
  1 cup sugar
  6 eggs, well beaten
  2 cups canned apple sauce

Line a 10-inch tube pan with double thickness of wax paper; then grease well. Cut up pineapple, citron, and cherries; mix in raisins and currants. Pour apple juice over fruits. Sift together flour, baking powder, salt, cinnamon, nutmeg and allspice. Cream olive oil and sugar; beat in eggs. Alternately add apple sauce and flour mixture to creamed mixture. Add fruit, a small amount at a time, mixing until thoroughly coated. Pour into prepared pan. Bake at 275°F. for 4 1/2 hours. Let cool in pan 15 to 20 minutes. Remove from pan; gently peel off wax paper. Cool thoroughly on wire rack. Wrap in foil. To serve, garnish cake with candied cherries and top each serving with warm apple sauce, if desired. Makes 7 1/4 pound cake; 20 slices.

CALORIES PER SERVING 360
GRAMS OF PROTEIN PER SERVING 4
GRAMS OF CARBOHYDRATE PER SERVING 57
GRAMS OF FAT PER SERVING 13

Crunchy Apples Caramel

1/2 cup walnuts
  2 tablespoons Spanish olive oil
  2 tablespoons butter or margarine
1 1/2 pounds (3 large) red apples, cored and sliced into rings
1/3 cup firmly packed light brown sugar
  3 tablespoons water
1/4 cup golden raisins
1/8 teaspoon nutmeg
     Dash salt

Saute walnuts in olive oil and butter in large skillet until lightly toasted; remove from pan. Fry apple rings on both sides until tender. Place apples and nuts in shallow serving dish; keep warm. Combine remaining ingredients in skillet; stir and heat until sugar dissolves and boils. Pour over apples and nuts. Serve warm. Makes 6 servings.

CALORIES PER SERVING 286
GRAMS OF PROTEIN PER SERVING 1
GRAMS OF CARBOHYDRATE PER SERVING 41
GRAMS OF FAT PER SERVING 14

Chocolate Fleck Cake

2¹/₄ cups sifted cake flour
1³/₄ cups sugar
   3 teaspoons baking powder
   1 teaspoon salt
¹/₂ cup Spanish olive oil
   5 egg yolks
³/₄ cup cold water
   2 teaspoons vanilla extract
   1 cup egg whites (7 or 8)
¹/₂ teaspoon cream of tartar
   3 squares unsweetened chocolate, grated

Sift flour with sugar, baking powder, and salt into mixing bowl. Make "well" in center. Add olive oil, egg yolks, water, and vanilla. Beat until smooth. Beat egg whites with cream of tartar until very stiff; fold in flour mixture and grated chocolate. Pour into ungreased 10-inch tube pan. Bake at 325°F. for 55 minutes. Raise temperature setting to 350°F. and continue baking 15 minutes or until top springs back when lightly touched. Invert pan on funnel or bottle. Cool thoroughly. Loosen cake from sides of pan with knife and invert onto serving platter. Makes 20 servings.

CALORIES PER SERVING 100
GRAMS OF PROTEIN PER SERVING 3
GRAMS OF CARBOHYDRATE PER SERVING 2
GRAMS OF FAT PER SERVING 9

Apple Lemon Nuggets

   1 package (3¹/₄ oz.) lemon pudding and pie filling
³/₄ cup sugar
   2 tablespoons lemon juice
   1 can (16 oz.) apple sauce
   2 egg yolks, beaten
   2 eggs whites, lightly beaten
1¹/₂ cups finely crushed unsalted soda crackers
   1 cup Spanish olive oil

In saucepan, mix pudding with sugar. Blend in lemon juice, apple sauce, and egg yolks. Bring to a boil over medium heat; then cook gently for 1 minute, stirring constantly. Lightly grease an 8-inch square pan with some of the olive oil, pour in lemon mixture, and refrigerate until set, about 4 hours. Cut into 36 squares, dip in beaten egg white, then coat with crumbs. Heat olive oil in skillet. Fry coated squares on both sides until lightly browned. Drain on paper towels. Serve warm, 2 or 3 squares per serving, topped with whipped cream, a fruit sauce, or fresh fruit. May also be served plain as appetizer or as an accompaniment to meat or fish entrees. Makes 36 nuggets.

CALORIES PER NUGGET 86
GRAMS OF PROTEIN PER NUGGET 0
GRAMS OF CARBOHYDRATE PER NUGGET 5
GRAMS OF FAT PER NUGGET 6

Giant Gingerbread

   1 can (16 oz.) apple sauce
   1 cup dark molasses
   1 cup raisins (optional)
   2 teaspoons baking soda
   3 cups sifted all-purpose flour
¹/₂ teaspoon salt
   2 teaspoons ginger
1¹/₂ teaspoons cinnamon
¹/₂ teaspoon cloves
   4 eggs
1¹/₃ cups sugar
²/₃ cup Spanish olive oil
   1 cup chopped nuts (optional)

Bring apple sauce to a boil. Stir in molasses, raisins and baking soda; cool to room temperature. Sift flour with salt and spices; set aside. Beat eggs with electric mixer until light in color. Gradually beat in sugar and continue beating until thick. Then gradually beat in olive oil. Alternately fold in flour mixture and apple sauce mixture. Fold in nuts. Pour into greased 10-inch tube pan. Bake at 325°F. for 1 hour and 15 minutes or until cake tester inserted in center comes out clean. Cool cake in pan 15 minutes. Then remove from pan and finish cooling on rack. Serve plain or with whipped cream or warm apple sauce. Makes 20 servings.

CALORIES PER SERVING 282
GRAMS OF PROTEIN PER SERVING 4
GRAMS OF CARBOHYDRATE PER SERVING 46
GRAMS OF FAT PER SERVING 9

Raisin Nut Cake

    1 cup boiling water
    1 cup raisins
1 1/2 teaspoons baking soda
    3 cups sifted all-purpose flour
    1 teaspoon salt
    3 eggs
    2 cups sugar
    1 cup Spanish olive oil
    2 teaspoons rum extract
    1 cup chopped walnuts or pecans

Pour boiling water over raisins. Let stand 5 minutes. Stir in baking soda. Sift flour with salt. Beat eggs with sugar; then beat in olive oil and rum extract. Stir in flour mixture alternately with raisin mixture. Fold in nuts. Pour into greased and floured 8-inch Bundt pan or 10-inch tube pan, or three 7-inch aluminum foil tube pans. Bake at 350°F. for 1 hour. Cool in pan 15 minutes; then remove from pan and cool on cake rack. Serve warm, topped with ice cream, if desired. Makes 20 servings.

CALORIES PER SERVING 218
GRAMS OF PROTEIN PER SERVING 3
GRAMS OF CARBOHYDRATE PER SERVING 16
GRAMS OF FAT PER SERVING 15

Irish Soda 'Cot Cake

    4 cups all-purpose flour
  1/3 cup sugar
    1 tablespoon double-acting baking powder
    1 teaspoon salt
  3/4 teaspoon baking soda
  1/3 cup Spanish olive oil
1 1/4 cups dark seedless raisins
  3/4 cup finely chopped dried apricots
1 1/2 to 2 teaspoons caraway seed
    2 eggs
1 1/2 cups buttermilk

Combine flour, sugar, baking powder, salt and baking soda in a large bowl. Add olive oil and toss until mixture resembles coarse crumbs. Stir in raisins, apricots and caraway seed. Beat eggs slightly; set aside 1 tablespoon. Combine remaining eggs and buttermilk; stir into flour mixture just until flour is moistened (dough will be sticky). Turn dough onto a well-floured surface. With floured hands, knead about 10 times. Shape dough into a ball; place in a greased 2-quart round, ovenproof casserole. Using a sharp knife, cut a cross, 4 inches long and 1/4 inch deep, in center of dough. Brush top with reserved egg. Bake in a 350°F. oven for 1 hour and 20 minutes, or until toothpick inserted in center comes out clean. Cool on wire rack 10 minutes; remove from casserole. Serve warm or cold. Makes 16 servings.

CALORIES PER SERVING 201
GRAMS OF PROTEIN PER SERVING 4
GRAMS OF CARBOHYDRATE PER SERVING 33
GRAMS OF FAT PER SERVING 5

Spicy Walnuts

Saute walnut halves in Spanish olive oil until golden; drain on absorbent paper. Sprinkle generously with salt, cinnamon, nutmeg or cloves. Serve with or use to garnish desserts.

Specialties from Spain

No matter where you go in Spain, olive oil is synonomous with cooking. Spanish cuisine makes the most of fresh fruits, vegetables, seafood and meats. Olive oil is used to bring out the natural flavors of the foods, since Spanish oil is light in flavor and texture. Try these Spanish specialties . . . close your eyes . . . take a deep breath . . . and suddenly you're moving in the world of Don Quixote!

Chuletas de Cerdo a la Aragonesa

1 clove garlic, crushed
1 teaspoon paprika
Pinch of cloves
1/4 cup Spanish olive oil
6 well-trimmed pork chops
2 tablespoons flour
1 teaspoon salt
1 tablespoon Spanish olive oil
1/2 cup chopped onion
1 tomato, peeled and chopped
2 tablespoons vinegar
1 cup chicken broth
Pinch of saffron

Combine garlic, paprika, cloves and 1/4 cup olive oil. Rub into chops; refrigerate several hours or overnight. Drain chops; coat with flour blended with salt. Brown quickly in 1 tablespoon olive oil. Remove chops and add onion to skillet. Cook until onions are tender. Add tomato, vinegar, broth and saffron; bring to a boil, reduce heat; replace chops in sauce, simmer until tender, about 25 minutes. Makes 6 servings.

CALORIES PER SERVING 379
GRAMS OF PROTEIN PER SERVING 24
GRAMS OF CARBOHYDRATE PER SERVING 4
GRAMS OF FAT PER SERVING 28

Estofado de Vaca Espanola (Beef Stew)

1 pound diced beef chuck
3 slices bacon, diced
2 cloves garlic, crushed
1 large onion, sliced
1/4 teaspoon sage
1/4 teaspoon marjoram
1 small bay leaf, crumbled
1/2 teaspoon paprika
1/2 teaspoon curry powder
3 medium tomatoes, diced
2 tablespoons vinegar
3/4 cup stock or bouillon
1/3 cup white wine
1 teaspoon salt
1/3 cup sliced pimiento-stuffed olives
2 tablespoons chopped parsley
4 medium potatoes, pared and cut in quarters

Combine beef, bacon, garlic and onion and cook over low heat until beef is browned on all sides. Add sage, marjoram, bay leaf, paprika, curry powder, tomatoes, vinegar, stock or bouillon, wine and salt; mix well. Cover and cook over low heat 1 hour, stirring occasionally. Add remaining ingredients; mix well. Cover and cook over low heat 40 minutes, stirring occasionally. Makes 4 servings.

CALORIES PER SERVING 676
GRAMS OF PROTEIN PER SERVING 32
GRAMS OF CARBOHYDRATE PER SERVING 29
GRAMS OF FAT PER SERVING 45

Paella

2 cloves garlic
1/4 cup Spanish olive oil
1/4 pound lean pork, diced, or 1 uncooked chicken breast, boned and cut in 1-inch pieces
1 pimiento, diced
1 medium onion, thinly sliced
1 cup uncooked rice
1 teaspoon salt
1/2 teaspoon saffron
2 1/2 cups boiling water
1 can (7 or 8 oz.) minced clams with juice
1 cup green beans, cut in 1-inch pieces, or peas
2 rock lobster tails, cut in thirds (undershell removed)
1 tablespoon minced parsley
1/2 pound cooked shrimp (optional)

In heavy 10-inch skillet or paella pan, heat garlic in olive oil until browned. Discard garlic and saute pork until lightly browned. Push pork aside and add pimiento and onion to skillet, cooking until onion is soft. Add rice, salt, and saffron; stir to coat rice with oil. Add boiling water, clams and juice, beans, and lobster pieces. Bring to a boil, lower heat, and cook uncovered for 15 minutes. (The mixture should boil steadily, but moderately.) Remove from heat. Stir in shrimp. Sprinkle parsley over top, cover and set aside for 10 minutes to allow for absorption of remaining liquid. Makes 6 servings.

CALORIES PER SERVING 245
GRAMS OF PROTEIN PER SERVING 16
GRAMS OF CARBOHYDRATE PER SERVING 21
GRAMS OF FAT PER SERVING 10

Codfish al Jerez

1 1/2 **pounds codfish, fresh or frozen**
2 **tablespoons Spanish olive oil**
3/4 **teaspoon salt**
1/4 **teaspoon oregano**
2 **tablespoons minced parsley**
2 **tablespoons slivered blanched almonds**
1/2 **cup dry sherry**

If frozen, defrost cod before cooking. Brush shallow baking dish with 1 tablespoon of the olive oil; place codfish in dish, sprinkle with salt and remaining olive oil. Sprinkle oregano, parsley, and almonds over top. Pour sherry over all. Bake at 350°F. for 25 to 30 minutes until fish flakes easily. Makes 4 servings.

CALORIES PER SERVING 233
GRAMS OF PROTEIN PER SERVING 26
GRAMS OF CARBOHYDRATE PER SERVING 0
GRAMS OF FAT PER SERVING 12

Pot Roast Aragonesa

3 or 4 **pound rump of veal, bottom round of beef, or chuck roast**
2 **tablespoons flour**
1 1/2 **teaspoons salt**
2 to 3 **tablespoons Spanish olive oil**
1 **large onion, sliced**
2 **cloves garlic, crushed**
2 **whole cloves**
1 **teaspoon cinnamon**
1 **bay leaf or 1 tablespoon minced parsley**
1 **tablespoon vinegar**
1 **tablespoon catsup**
2 **cups water**
1/2 **ounce bitter chocolate, grated**

Dust meat with flour which has been mixed with 1/2 teaspoon of the salt. Heat olive oil in Dutch oven or in casserole which can be used on top of stove and brown the meat. Remove meat, add onions and garlic and cook until yellow; replace meat and add remaining ingredients except chocolate. Cover with tight-fitting lid and simmer 2 1/2 to 3 hours until meat is very tender. Remove meat to platter, add more water to pot if necessary to make 2 cups sauce. Add

chocolate. Cook, stirring, until sauce is thickened. Serve sauce with roast. Makes 10 servings.

CALORIES PER SERVING 273
GRAMS OF PROTEIN PER SERVING 32
GRAMS OF CARBOHYDRATE PER SERVING 3
GRAMS OF FAT PER SERVING 13

Gazpacho Andaluz

1/4 **pound day-old Italian or French bread or hard rolls, cubed (1 quart)**
Water
1 1/2 **cups pared and diced cucumber**
1 **medium green pepper, seeded and cut up**
2 **cloves garlic**
2 **teaspoons salt**
1/2 **cup Spanish olive oil**
1/4 **cup wine vinegar**
2 **pounds fresh ripe tomatoes, seeded and cubed**
Ice cubes

Accompaniments:
sliced pimiento-stuffed olives
diced cucumber
chopped scallions or onion
diced tomatoes
chopped green pepper
croutons fried in olive oil
crisp crumbled bacon
sliced toasted almonds
chopped hard-cooked egg

Place bread in shallow dish; add water 1 inch deep. Let bread soak, turning once. Meanwhile in electric blender combine cucumber, green pepper, garlic, salt, olive oil and vinegar, blend smooth. Add 1/2 the bread and blend smooth. Pour into a bowl. Blend remaining bread and tomatoes and add to mixture in bowl. Taste and season with more salt and vinegar, if desired. Chill thoroughly. When ready to serve, place 1 or 2 ice cubes in each bowl of soup. Serve with the accompaniments. Makes 7 servings.

CALORIES PER SERVING 390
GRAMS OF PROTEIN PER SERVING 10
GRAMS OF CARBOHYDRATE PER SERVING 25
GRAMS OF FAT PER SERVING 28

Rockfish a la Ferezana

¼ **cup pignolas (pine nuts)**
¼ **cup Spanish olive oil**
½ **cup thinly sliced leek (white part only)**
¼ **pound mushrooms, coarsely chopped**
2 **medium carrots, finely grated**
½ **cup raisins**
½ **medium red or green pepper, chopped**
1 **cup chopped cooked shrimp (about ½ pound raw)**
½ **cup small whole pimiento-stuffed olives**
Salt and pepper
3 **to 4 pound striped bass, cleaned**
3 **tablespoons butter, melted**
3 **tablespoons Spanish olive oil**
½ **cup brandy**
Salt and pepper

In saucepan saute pignolas in ¼ cup olive oil until lightly browned. Remove pignolas with slotted spoon and set aside. In same pan saute leek and mushrooms until tender but not browned. Add carrots, raisins and pepper; cover and cook over low heat 5 minutes. Stir in shrimp and olives and season to taste with salt and pepper; set aside. Place fish in large shallow roasting pan. Pour melted butter, olive oil and ¼ cup of the brandy over the bass; sprinkle with salt and pepper. Bake uncovered in 400°F. oven 15 minutes. Spoon olive mixture over the fish; then sprinkle with pignolas. Heat remaining brandy, ignite and pour over olive mixture. Basting occasionally, bake 15 to 20 minutes longer, or until fish flakes easily with a fork. Serve with parsley potatoes. Makes 4 to 6 servings.

```
CALORIES PER SERVING ............................ 1080
GRAMS OF PROTEIN PER SERVING ................. 77
GRAMS OF CARBOHYDRATE PER SERVING ........... 45
GRAMS OF FAT PER SERVING ...................... 65
```

Codfish a la Riojana

2 **pounds codfish steaks, fresh or frozen**
½ **cup Spanish olive oil**
3 **medium or 2 large onions, sliced**
3 **large potatoes, very thinly sliced**
4 **pimientos, drained, sliced**
1½ **teaspoons salt**
¼ **cup white wine or water**
¼ **cup minced parsley**

If frozen codfish is used, defrost before cooking. Place olive oil in heavy skillet over moderate heat (or electric skillet set at 220°). Add onions, potatoes, pimientos and 1 teaspoon of the salt to olive oil. Cover and simmer 1 hour without allowing to brown; stir occasionally to prevent sticking. Spoon off excess olive oil. Place codfish on bottom of skillet, top with vegetables. Add parsley and wine. Cover and continue cooking over low heat until fish flakes easily (about 20 minutes). Makes 6 servings.

```
CALORIES PER SERVING ............................ 440
GRAMS OF PROTEIN PER SERVING ................... 36
GRAMS OF CARBOHYDRATE PER SERVING ........... 13
GRAMS OF FAT PER SERVING ....................... 25
```

Menestra of Lamb

2½ **pounds boneless lamb, cubed**
¼ **cup Spanish olive oil**
3 **scallions, chopped**
1 **can (16 oz.) peeled tomatoes**
1 **clove garlic, crushed**
⅓ **cup dry white wine**
1 **cup water or stock**
1 **teaspoon salt**
Dash black pepper
¼ **pound (1 cup) cut green beans**
1 **package (10 oz.) frozen peas; or 1 package frozen artichoke hearts**
12 **asparagus spears, cooked**
3 **hard-cooked eggs**

In large casserole or skillet, brown meat in hot olive oil. Push aside and add scallions; cook until these are soft. Add tomatoes, garlic and wine; simmer 5 minutes. Add water, salt and pepper; bring to a boil, then lower heat and simmer until meat is tender, about 1 hour. Add beans and peas; cook until tender, about 10 minutes. Serve, garnishing with hot asparagus spears and eggs cut in wedges. Makes 8 servings.

```
CALORIES PER SERVING ............................ 255
GRAMS OF PROTEIN PER SERVING ................... 22
GRAMS OF CARBOHYDRATE PER SERVING ........... 8
GRAMS OF FAT PER SERVING ....................... 14
```

Pisto Manchego

1/4 cup Spanish olive oil
1 medium onion, sliced
1 or 2 cloves garlic
1 can (14 oz.) artichoke hearts
1 small eggplant, cubed
3 tomatoes, peeled, chopped; or 1 can (16 oz.) tomatoes
1 package (9 oz.) frozen lima beans
3/4 teaspoon salt
1/4 cup minced parsley

Place olive oil in large heavy skillet or deep pot, add onion and garlic, cook until soft; mash garlic, or remove and discard. Drain artichoke hearts, cut in half lengthwise. Add artichoke hearts, eggplant, tomatoes, lima beans, salt and parsley. Cover and simmer until vegetables are tender, about 30 minutes. Serve hot or cold. Makes 6 servings.

CALORIES PER SERVING 350
GRAMS OF PROTEIN PER SERVING 5
GRAMS OF CARBOHYDRATE PER SERVING 20
GRAMS OF FAT PER SERVING 9

Carmelite Soup

1 pound dried chick peas
Water
6 whole cloves
6 whole peppercorns
4 bay leaves
2 tablespoons onion powder
1 1/2 teaspoons salt
1 1/2 quarts chicken broth
1 1/2 cups sliced carrots
1 1/2 cups diced potatoes
1 1/2 cups diced cabbage
2 tablespoons Spanish olive oil
2 tablespoons parsley flakes
1/4 teaspoon ground black pepper
2 hard-cooked eggs, sliced
Paprika

Soak chick peas in 2 quarts of water for 12 hours or longer. Drain. In a large saucepan combine chick peas with 1 quart of water. Add cloves, peppercorns and bay leaves tied in cheesecloth bag. Stir in onion powder and salt. Bring to boil. Cover and cook 2 hours or until tender (add more water if needed). Meanwhile, in another saucepan combine chicken broth, carrots, potatoes and cabbage; bring to a boil. Reduce heat, cover and simmer 30 minutes or until vegetables are tender. Remove and discard spice bag from chick pea mixture. Then puree with olive oil in blender. Stir into vegetable mixture. Heat thoroughly. Stir in parsley flakes and pepper. Serve in soup bowls. Float sliced egg over each portion. Sprinkle with paprika. Makes 12 servings.

CALORIES PER SERVING 195
GRAMS OF PROTEIN PER SERVING 10
GRAMS OF CARBOHYDRATE PER SERVING 28
GRAMS OF FAT PER SERVING 5

Sole Valencia

1/3 cup diced onion flakes
2 tablespoons sweet pepper flakes
1/4 teaspoon instant minced garlic
1/3 cup water
2 tablespoons Spanish olive oil, divided
1 can (16 oz.) tomatoes, broken up
1 can (8 oz.) tomato sauce
1 bay leaf
1/8 teaspoon whole saffron, crumbled
2 pounds filet of sole
3 tablespoons flour
3 tablespoons dry bread crumbs
1 1/2 teaspoons salt
1/4 teaspoon pepper
1/2 cup Spanish olive oil

Rehydrate onion and pepper flakes and minced garlic in water for 10 minutes. In a saucepan heat 2 tablespoons olive oil. Add onion, peppers and garlic; saute 5 minutes. Stir in tomatoes, tomato sauce, bay leaf and saffron. Cook, stirring occasionally for 10 minutes. Dredge fish with flour and bread crumbs seasoned with salt and pepper. In a large skillet heat remaining olive oil. Add fish, a few filets at a time, and fry until golden on both sides. Remove to serving dish. Spoon sauce over fish and serve. Makes 8 servings.

CALORIES PER SERVING 499
GRAMS OF PROTEIN PER SERVING 21
GRAMS OF CARBOHYDRATE PER SERVING 49
GRAMS OF FAT PER SERVING 23

Spanish Cocido

    2 pounds boned chuck or breast of veal
 1/4 cup Spanish olive oil
    3 or 4 large onions, chopped or sliced
    2 cloves garlic, minced
    2 tomatoes, quartered
 1/2 cup minced parsley
    1 cup chopped ham
    1 ham bone
    4 chicken wings
    1 pound chick peas (garbanzos)
    3 quarts cold water
    1 tablespoon salt, or to taste
    4 carrots, cubed

The meat is usually placed in a heavy pot or Dutch oven in a single piece, but may be cut into chunks if preferred. Brown in olive oil over high heat. Lower heat, add remaining ingredients and bring slowly to a boil; then cover and simmer very gently over very low heat for 4 to 5 hours. Add more liquid as it cooks, if needed; the chick peas must be well-covered throughout the cooking period (but they need not be soaked before cooking). Makes 12 servings.

Variations: The authentic Spanish Cocido is made with sausage, and best of all is chorizo sausage, made of pure pork, garlic, olive oil and paprika. If American sausage is added, it must be cooked separately and well-drained before adding to the pot. Sausage is used in place of ham.

Instead of a ham bone, a veal knuckle is excellent. And instead of chopped ham, lean cubes of bacon may be used.

Instead of 4 chicken wings, an entire stewing chicken (cut up) may be used; in this case, use less beef or veal.

Sometimes, instead of searing the meat and sauteeing the onion in olive oil, everything is placed in the pot at once, without previously browning, including the olive oil. In northern Spain, the meat is parboiled briefly first, this water thrown away, then fresh water and all the other ingredients are added.

Sweet potatoes are sometimes added to the Cocido, especially in southern Spain. In northern Spain, white potatoes are more likely to go into the pot.

CALORIES PER SERVING 392
GRAMS OF PROTEIN PER SERVING 20
GRAMS OF CARBOHYDRATE PER SERVING 28
GRAMS OF FAT PER SERVING 22

Giralda Rice with Chicken and Sausage

    1 pound chorizo or garlic flavored
         sausage, sliced
    1 medium eggplant, cut in 1/2-inch slices
    1 teaspoon salt
 1/2 cup Spanish olive oil
    2 large tomatoes, peeled and chopped
    1 medium onion, chopped
 1 1/2 cups uncooked rice
    2 medium green peppers, chopped
 1/4 cup chopped parsley
 1/4 teaspoon thyme
 1/8 teaspoon pepper
    3 cups chicken bouillon
    3 cups diced, cooked chicken
 1/2 cup sliced pimiento-stuffed olives
    2 large tomatoes, peeled and sliced
 1/2 cup whole pimiento-stuffed olives
    3 ounces Gruyere cheese, grated

In large skillet, brown sausage. Remove fat and drain sausage on paper towels. Sprinkle eggplant with salt, and fry in 1/3 cup of the olive oil; remove and drain. In same skillet, combine remaining olive oil, chopped tomatoes, onion and rice; saute 2 minutes. Mix in sausage, green pepper, parsley, thyme, pepper and bouillon. Cover and boil gently 20 minutes or until rice is tender, stirring occasionally. Stir in chicken and sliced olives. Turn into paella pan or 3 1/2 quart oven-proof serving dish. Overlap eggplant and tomato slices around edges of dish. Place whole olives in center. Sprinkle cheese on top. Broil 6 inches from source of heat for 4 minutes or until cheese melts and browns lightly. Makes 6 servings.

CALORIES PER SERVING 721
GRAMS OF PROTEIN PER SERVING 33
GRAMS OF CARBOHYDRATE PER SERVING 39
GRAMS OF FAT PER SERVING 48

International Favorites

Olive oil has influenced the cuisine of
any country where it is produced . . . . and all the
neighboring lands as well. Even Chinese
recipes, which use sesame oil, take on new
meaning when Spanish olive oil is substituted,
as we have done in this section. A world tour is as
close as your kitchen. Experiment. Enjoy!

Orancini (Little Oranges)
(Italy)

      3 cups hot cooked rice
    1/2 cup butter
      3 tablespoons grated Parmesan cheese
    1/2 pound ground beef
      2 tablespoons Spanish olive oil
      1 clove garlic, minced
    1/2 small onion, minced
    1/4 pound mushrooms, sliced
      1 cup spaghetti sauce
      2 egg yolks
      1 egg, beaten
      1 cup bread crumbs
         Spanish olive oil

Mix hot rice with butter and cheese; set aside to cool. Meanwhile, brown ground beef in olive oil. Then add garlic, onion, and mushrooms and cook until tender. Stir in spaghetti sauce. Simmer, uncovered, for 30 minutes. Drain and reserve the tomato liquid left after simmering. Add this reserved liquid with the beaten egg yolks to rice mixture. Place about 1/4 cup rice mixture in one hand and flatten out. Top with a tablespoon of meat mixture; then shape rice mixture around the meat . . . to make a rice ball with a meat filling. Dip rice balls in beaten egg, coat with crumbs, and fry in olive oil (about 1 inch deep in pan), turning until golden on all sides. Makes 6 servings.

CALORIES PER SERVING 566
GRAMS OF PROTEIN PER SERVING 15
GRAMS OF CARBOHYDRATE PER SERVING 34
GRAMS OF FAT PER SERVING 40

Tostadas with Chicken
(Mexico)

     12 tortillas, canned or frozen
    1/2 cup Spanish olive oil
      2 cans (16 oz. *each*) kidney beans, drained
    1/4 teaspoon garlic powder
         Salt and Pepper
         Tabasco sauce
      1 can (12 oz.) boned chicken, or leftover
         chicken or turkey, preferably white meat
      2 small avocados, peeled and sliced
      1 cup grated Parmesan cheese
      1 medium head iceberg lettuce, shredded
         Salsa

Fry each tortilla in hot olive oil about 2 minutes; drain on paper towels. Drain off all but 2 tablespoons olive oil; add beans and garlic powder. Cook and mash until a thick paste forms and beans are dry enough to turn out of skillet like an omelet. Add salt and pepper to taste. Spread bean mixture on tortillas; sprinkle with Tabasco. Top with chicken, avocado, cheese, lettuce and Salsa. Makes 6 servings.

CALORIES PER SERVING 782
GRAMS OF PROTEIN PER SERVING 37
GRAMS OF CARBOHYDRATE PER SERVING 68
GRAMS OF FAT PER SERVING 42

Spicy Skewered Lamb
(India)

      2 pounds lamb, cut in 1 1/2-inch cubes
    1/2 cup lemon juice
    1/4 cup Spanish olive oil
      2 tablespoons grated onion
      2 tablespoons chili powder
      1 tablespoon ground coriander
      1 tablespoon powdered ginger
      1 clove garlic, mashed
      2 teaspoons turmeric
      3 teaspoons salt
      6 tomatoes, cut in wedges
      3 large onions, cut in wedges
      3 green peppers, sliced in 1/2-inch strips
      1 pound of fresh mushrooms, stems
         trimmed off

Marinate lamb overnight in mixture of lemon juice, olive oil and seasonings in refrigerator. Alternate lamb, tomatoes, onions, green peppers and mushroom caps on skewers. Broil about 4 inches from heat source turning and basting with marinade occasionally, until brown on all sides. Serve with buckwheat groats. Makes 6 servings.

CALORIES PER SERVING 299
GRAMS OF PROTEIN PER SERVING 23
GRAMS OF CARBOHYDRATE PER SERVING 18
GRAMS OF FAT PER SERVING 15

Djaj Bimarak Assaitoun
(Chicken with Olive Oil)
(Morocco)

2 chickens, about 2 1/2 pounds *each*,
   quartered
1 teaspoon powdered saffron
1/2 cup butter
1 cup Spanish olive oil
4 cups chicken broth
3/4 teaspoon tarragon
1/2 cup chopped parsley
2 large bay leaves
2 whole cloves
1/2 cup lemon juice
3/4 teaspoon salt
3/4 teaspoon pepper
2 1/4 cups small green Spanish olives, unpitted
1 1/4 cups brown Mediterranean olives, unpitted
4 pickled lemons

Rub skin of chicken pieces with saffron.
Brown in deep pan in butter and olive oil,
turning frequently. Add chicken broth, tarragon, chopped parsley, bay leaves, cloves,
lemon juice, salt, pepper and 1/4 cup *each*
of Spanish and Mediterranean olives.
Cover, simmer 1 hour or until chicken is
tender. Remove to heated serving dish;
skim off 3/4 cup fat; reduce liquid by one-
fourth to use as sauce. Top chicken pieces
with 2 cups Spanish olives, 1 cup
Mediterranean olives, and 4 pickled lemons. Serve sauce on the side for chickens
and dipping bread — preferably the flat
Arabic kind. Makes 6 servings.

Pickled Lemons

4 large lemons
2 1/2 cups wine vinegar
1/2 cup Spanish olive oil
1 teaspoon coarse, ground salt
7 peppercorns, crushed

Cut lemons into 3 wedges each; put into
deep glass jar. Add wine vinegar, olive oil,
salt and peppercorns. Cover; refrigerate 2
days, drain.

```
CALORIES PER SERVING ............................ 1206
GRAMS OF PROTEIN PER SERVING ................... 57
GRAMS OF CARBOHYDRATE PER SERVING .......... 24
GRAMS OF FAT PER SERVING ....................... 104
```

Frijoles (Refried Beans)
(Mexico)

1 tablespoon Spanish olive oil
2 cans (16 oz. *each*) kidney beans, drained
1 teaspoon salt
1 cup grated Cheddar cheese
1 head iceberg lettuce, shredded
1 avocado, peeled and sliced

Heat olive oil in skillet; add beans and salt.
Cook and mash until a thick paste forms,
and beans are dry enough to turn out of
skillet like an omelet. Press into a small
greased loaf pan. At serving time, unmold
on platter on bed of lettuce. Sprinkle cheese
over top. Garnish with avocado slices.
Makes 6 servings.

```
CALORIES PER SERVING ............................ 341
GRAMS OF PROTEIN PER SERVING ................... 18
GRAMS OF CARBOHYDRATE PER SERVING .......... 36
GRAMS OF FAT PER SERVING ....................... 14
```

Cantonese Pork Chops
(China)

6 loin pork chops, 1-inch thick
2 tablespoons Spanish olive oil
1 can (30 oz.) apricot halves
1/2 cup water
2 1/2 tablespoons soy sauce
1 large clove garlic, crushed
1/2 teaspoon powdered ginger
1 can (8 oz.) water chestnuts, sliced
5 scallions, sliced
2 cups diagonally sliced celery
   Salt and pepper
3 cups hot cooked rice mixed with parsley

Brown chops on both sides in hot olive oil
in large skillet. Pour off excess oil. Drain
syrup from apricots into skillet and add
water, soy sauce, garlic and ginger. Cover
and simmer 35 minutes; if necessary, add
more water during cooking period. Add
water chestnuts, scallions and celery; cook
about 5 minutes more or until celery is tender. Add apricots and cook just until heated
through. Season to taste with salt and pepper. Serve with rice. Makes 6 servings.

```
CALORIES PER SERVING ............................ 752
GRAMS OF PROTEIN PER SERVING ................... 31
GRAMS OF CARBOHYDRATE PER SERVING .......... 45
GRAMS OF FAT PER SERVING ....................... 49
```

Rice Oriental
(Indonesia)

- 3 tablespoons Spanish olive oil
- 1 cup uncooked rice
- 1/2 cup chopped onion
- 1/4 teaspoon ground ginger
- 2 cups chicken broth or bouillon
- 1 cup diced dried apricots
- 1/3 cup dark seedless raisins
- 1/2 cup chopped celery
- 1/2 cup salted peanuts
  - Salt

Heat olive oil in large skillet; add rice and onion and saute until golden brown. Add ginger, chicken broth, apricots, raisins, and celery. Simmer, covered, about 12 to 14 minutes or until rice is tender. Mix peanuts into rice mixture and season to taste with salt. Serve as an accompaniment to roast pork or poultry. Makes 6 servings.

```
CALORIES PER SERVING ............................. 334
GRAMS OF PROTEIN PER SERVING ................... 9
GRAMS OF CARBOHYDRATE PER SERVING ........... 39
GRAMS OF FAT PER SERVING ........................ 16
```

Walnut-Rice Salad
(Turkey)

- 2 cups water
- 1 teaspoon salt
- 1/2 teaspoon oregano
- 1/2 teaspoon grated lemon peel
- 1 cup uncooked rice
- 1 cup chopped celery
- 2 tablespoons finely chopped onion
- 3/4 cup coarsely chopped, toasted walnuts
- 1/4 cup sliced pimiento-stuffed green olives
  - Lemon Dressing
- 1 head iceberg lettuce
  - Yogurt

Heat water to boiling with salt, oregano and lemon peel; add rice, cover and cook for 20 minutes, or until water is absorbed. Cool thoroughly. Add celery, onion, walnuts and olives. Pour Lemon Dressing over all and toss lightly. Serve on bed of crisp lettuce. Top with a small spoonful of yogurt. Makes 6 servings.

Lemon Dressing:

- 1/4 cup Spanish olive oil
- 2 tablespoons lemon juice
- 1/2 teaspoon salt
- 1/8 teaspoon pepper

Combine ingredients and shake together or beat well.

```
CALORIES PER SERVING ............................. 401
GRAMS OF PROTEIN PER SERVING ................... 7
GRAMS OF CARBOHYDRATE PER SERVING ........... 25
GRAMS OF FAT PER SERVING ........................ 31
```

Hungarian Fried Noodles and Cabbage Budapest Style
(Hungary)

- 1 cup minced onion
- 1 clove garlic, crushed
- 1/2 cup Spanish olive oil
- 1 pound medium noodles
  - Water
  - Salt
- 1 medium head of cabbage, shredded
- 10 slices bacon, diced
- 2 cups large curd cottage cheese
- 1 cup dairy sour cream
- 1/2 teaspoon salt
- 1/8 teaspoon pepper
- 1 tablespoon caraway seed (optional)

In a large skillet saute onion and garlic in olive oil until tender. Cook noodles in boiling salted water until not quite tender, about 2 to 3 minutes; drain. Add the noodles to the onion and garlic mixture. Fry slowly for 5 minutes, tossing the noodles. Boil cabbage in salted water until crisp-tender, 2 to 3 minutes; drain well. In separate pan, fry bacon until crisp. Remove bacon pieces; drain. Fry cabbage in bacon fat. Add cottage cheese, sour cream, salt, pepper and caraway seed to the cabbage mixture; mix well. Combine noodles and cabbage in 2-quart baking dish. Sprinkle bacon pieces over top. Bake at 300°F. for 20 minutes. Makes 6 servings.

```
CALORIES PER SERVING ............................. 893
GRAMS OF PROTEIN PER SERVING ................... 24
GRAMS OF CARBOHYDRATE PER SERVING ........... 72
GRAMS OF FAT PER SERVING ........................ 56
```

Macaroni with Lamb Stew, Greek Style (Greece)

6 pounds shoulder of lamb, cubed
1/4 cup Spanish olive oil
6 medium onions, sliced
3 cans (8 oz. *each*) tomato sauce
3/4 cup water
1 tablespoon salt
1½ teaspoons marjoram
3/4 teaspoon pepper
2 small eggplants, cubed
3 large green peppers, diced
1½ pounds okra, trimmed, or cut green beans
6 medium tomatoes, peeled and cut in wedges
3 tablespoons salt
8 quarts boiling water
6 cups elbow macaroni (1½ lb.)

Brown lamb in olive oil in Dutch oven or large pot; drain off all but 2 tablespoons of the drippings. Add onions to lamb; saute about 7 minutes. Stir in tomato sauce, 3/4 cup water, 1 tablespoon salt, the marjoram and pepper. Cover and simmer for 45 minutes. Add eggplant, green pepper and okra. Simmer 30 minutes or until lamb and vegetables are tender. Add tomatoes; cook uncovered for 5 to 10 minutes, stirring occasionally. Add 3 tablespoons salt to rapidly boiling water. Gradually add macaroni so that water continues to boil. Cook, uncovered, stirring occasionally until tender; drain. Serve stew over macaroni. Makes 12 servings.

CALORIES PER SERVING 619
GRAMS OF PROTEIN PER SERVING 40
GRAMS OF CARBOHYDRATE PER SERVING 70
GRAMS OF FAT PER SERVING 20

Shrimp with Coconut (Polynesian)

1 1/2 pounds shrimp
 1/2 teaspoon dried mint leaves
   1 cup flaked coconut
 3/4 cup diced green pepper
   4 cloves garlic
1 1/2 teaspoons ground cumin
   2 tablespoons lemon juice
   1 teaspoon salt
 1/3 cup Spanish olive oil
 3/4 cup diced onion
   3 cups hot cooked rice

Shell, devein and wash shrimp; drain on paper towels and set aside. Using fine blade in grinder, or high speed on electric blender, make a paste of mint, coconut, green pepper, garlic, cumin, lemon juice and salt. Heat olive oil in large skillet over moderate heat, add paste mixture and fry gently for about 3 minutes. Stir in shrimp and onions; cover and gently fry for 8 to 10 minutes or until shrimp are tender. Do not overcook. Serve with hot fluffy rice. Makes 6 servings.

CALORIES PER SERVING 364
GRAMS OF PROTEIN PER SERVING 23
GRAMS OF CARBOHYDRATE PER SERVING 24
GRAMS OF FAT PER SERVING 19

Huevos Mexicanos (Mexican Eggs) (Mexico)

1 1/2 cups chopped onion
1 1/2 cups chopped green pepper
   1 clove garlic, crushed
 3/4 cup Spanish olive oil
   1 tablespoon chili powder
 1/2 teaspoon salt
 1/4 teaspoon oregano
   9 slices white bread, trimmed and cut into cubes
   6 eggs
   6 tablespoons tomato juice
 1/2 cup shredded Cheddar cheese

Cook onion, green pepper and garlic in olive oil in skillet until soft. Stir in seasonings; simmer 5 minutes. Mix in bread cubes. Spoon into six 6-ounce baking dishes, pressing firmly in bottom and up sides. Break an egg into center of each. Spoon 1 tablespoon tomato juice over each egg; sprinkle with cheese. Bake at 350°F. for 20 to 25 minutes, or until eggs set. Serve hot. Makes 6 servings.

CALORIES PER SERVING 496
GRAMS OF PROTEIN PER SERVING 13
GRAMS OF CARBOHYDRATE PER SERVING 24
GRAMS OF FAT PER SERVING 37

Spiedino Alla Romano
(Italy)

1/2 cup Spanish olive oil
4 cloves garlic, crushed or minced
1 can (2 oz.) flat anchovies, drained and chopped
1/4 cup minced parsley
1/4 loaf Italian bread
1 package (8 oz.) Mozzarella cheese

Heat olive oil in small frying pan over moderate heat. Add garlic and cook about one minute; do not brown. Add anchovies and simmer over very low heat for two to three minutes. Remove from heat and stir in parsley. Cut bread into 6 slices about 1/3 inch thick. Remove crusts and brush both sides of bread with some of the liquid part of the sauce. Cut cheese into 5 slices. Alternate the 6 slices of bread with 5 slices cheese, beginning and ending with bread onto two metal skewers. Place each skewer in a heatproof baking dish. Pour remainder of sauce over tops. Bake at 450°F. for about 12 minutes, or until cheese is melted and bread is crusty and browned. Remove skewers and serve immediately. Makes 2 servings.

CALORIES PER SERVING 1125
GRAMS OF PROTEIN PER SERVING 36
GRAMS OF CARBOHYDRATE PER SERVING 30
GRAMS OF FAT PER SERVING 94

Khorsht Bademjoon
(Curried Eggplant)
(Persia)

2 medium eggplants, about 1 pound *each*
1 tablespoon salt
1 1/2 pounds lamb or beef cubes
3 tablespoons Spanish olive oil
1/2 cup chopped onion
3 cups water
1/2 teaspoon salt
1/2 teaspoon powdered saffron
1/4 teaspoon pepper
3 tablespoons freshly squeezed lemon juice
1/2 can (6 oz.) tomato paste
1/2 cup Spanish olive oil
1 can (17 oz.) whole peeled tomatoes, drained
3 cups hot cooked rice

Cut eggplants into 1/2-inch slices; peel. Sprinkle with salt, place in a bowl, and let stand 1 hour (to draw out some of water). Meanwhile, saute meat in 3 tablespoons olive oil until browned. Add chopped onion and continue cooking until onion is tender, but not browned. Stir in water, bring to a boil, cover and simmer for 30 minutes. Stir in 1/2 teaspoon salt, saffron, pepper, lemon juice and tomato paste. Cover, simmer until meat is tender and sauce has thickened (about 2 1/2 hours). Meanwhile, drain eggplant slices and saute in 1/2 cup olive oil in a skillet, adding more olive oil to skillet if necessary. Cook until browned on both sides. Add eggplant slices and canned tomatoes to pan with cooked meat in it. Cover and continue cooking about 20 minutes (or until eggplant is tender but not mushy). Serve over rice. Makes 4 servings.

CALORIES PER SERVING 733
GRAMS OF PROTEIN PER SERVING 28
GRAMS OF CARBOHYDRATE PER SERVING 55
GRAMS OF FAT PER SERVING 45

Moyin-Moyin
(Nigeria)

 1 cup blackeye beans
 1 medium onion
 1 hot pepper
1/2 cup water
1/2 cup Spanish olive oil
 2 eggs
1/4 cup tomato paste
    Salt to taste (approx. 1 1/2 teaspoons)

Soak beans in water for 30 to 40 minutes. Remove skins. Grind beans, onion and hot pepper until very smooth. (A blender may be used.) Add remaining ingredients and beat for 5 minutes. Fill greased muffin pans to within a quarter-inch of top. Cover muffin pans tightly with aluminum foil. Put 3 cups water in large pan. Set muffin pans in pan, cover and steam for 40 to 45 minutes. Makes 12 individual Moyin-moyin.

Variation: Moyin-moyin oleme-meje (translation — Moyin-moyin with seven souls). Prepare basic Moyin-moyin. Fill greased muffin pans half full. Place a small piece of hard-cooked egg, minced meat, cooked shrimp and fish, and uncooked liver, kidney and heart in each Moyin-moyin. Top with remaining mixture and proceed as described above.

CALORIES PER SERVING 139
GRAMS OF PROTEIN PER SERVING 3
GRAMS OF CARBOHYDRATE PER SERVING 8
GRAMS OF FAT PER SERVING 10

Shish Kebab
(Turkish Lamb Kabobs)
(Turkey)

1 1/4 pounds of lamb, cut into cubes
1/2 cup yogurt
1/2 teaspoon crushed dried mint
1/4 teaspoon black pepper
1/4 teaspoon salt
 1 tablespoon grated onion
 1 small eggplant cut into 16 cubes
1/4 cup Spanish olive oil
 1 teaspoon salt
1/8 teaspoon pepper
 1 clove garlic, crushed

Marinate lamb in mixture of yogurt, mint, pepper, salt and onion for several hours. Refrigerate. Separately marinate eggplant cubes in seasoned olive oil. Remove meat from yogurt marinade, scrape off yogurt, brush with olive oil. Place eggplant and lamb cubes alternately on barbecue skewers, adding quartered tomatoes, if desired. Broil 4 inches from charcoal fire, occasionally brushing meat with olive oil until meat is well browned and eggplant delicately browned, about 12 minutes. Serves 4.

CALORIES PER SERVING 292
GRAMS OF PROTEIN PER SERVING 19
GRAMS OF CARBOHYDRATE PER SERVING 8
GRAMS OF FAT PER SERVING 20

Kicklach (Egg Cookies)
(Israel)

 3 eggs
1/2 cup Spanish olive oil
 3 tablespoons sugar
 1 cup all-purpose flour
1/8 teaspoon salt

Combine eggs, olive oil and sugar in a mixing bowl; beat at highest speed for 15 minutes. Add flour and salt and beat on high for an additional 5 minutes. Drop by tablespoon several inches apart on greased cookie sheet. Bake in preheated 350°F. oven for 30 minutes. Makes approximately 24 cookies.

CALORIES PER COOKIE 75
GRAMS OF PROTEIN PER COOKIE 1
GRAMS OF CARBOHYDRATE PER COOKIE 5
GRAMS OF FAT PER COOKIE 5

CALORIES PER SERVING 334
GRAMS OF PROTEIN PER SERVING 11
GRAMS OF CARBOHYDRATE PER SERVING 10
GRAMS OF FAT PER SERVING 29

Fruit Kebab Salad
(Middle East)

1 large or 2 medium heads iceberg lettuce
1 or 2 oranges
1 red apple
   Dates

Core, rinse and drain lettuce thoroughly. Refrigerate in lettuce crisper or plastic bag. Cut lettuce into 8 serving-size wedges. Remove rind and white layer from oranges; slice across segments into 1/4-inch thick slices. Cut apple into wedges, remove core and dip into fruit juice to prevent browning. For each kebab, skewer 2 apple wedges, and 1 orange slice centered with a date. Spike into lettuce wedge; drizzle 2-3 tablespoons dressing over each serving. Makes 8 servings.

Dressing

   1 cup Spanish olive oil
1/3 cup lemon juice
   2 tablespoons minced parsley
   2 teaspoons grated fresh ginger root
1 1/2 teaspoons sugar
1 1/2 teaspoons salt
   1 teaspoon mustard seed, cracked
3/4 teaspoon curry powder
1/4 teaspoon garlic powder

In pint jar combine all ingredients and shake to mix. Store overnight to develop flavors. Makes about 1 1/2 cups dressing.

CALORIES PER SERVING 327
GRAMS OF PROTEIN PER SERVING 0
GRAMS OF CARBOHYDRATE PER SERVING 20
GRAMS OF FAT PER SERVING 28

Grecian Style Salad
(Greece)

   1 head iceberg lettuce
1/2 cup radish slices
1/2 cup chopped green onion
1/3 cup Spanish olive oil
   2 tablespoons lemon juice
   2 teaspoons sugar
1/2 teaspoon salt
   Few dashes pepper
   4 ounces Feta or Romano cheese
   1 can (2 oz.) flat anchovy fillets, drained
   About 2/3 cup whole pitted ripe olives
   Crumbled dry oregano

Core, rinse and drain lettuce; chill in plastic bag or lettuce crisper. Cut head in half lengthwise; place cut sides down on board and shred crosswise; then chop to yield 5 cups. Combine chopped lettuce with radishes and onion in salad bowl. Mix olive oil, lemon juice, sugar and salt with pepper to taste. Toss with lettuce. Crumble cheese coarsely and sprinkle over salad near rim of bowl. Wrap each anchovy around an olive and place inside ring of cheese. Sprinkle oregano over all. Toss salad before serving. Makes 6 servings.

Spicy Baked Fish
(Polynesian)

     1 whole fish (2 to 2¹/₂ lb.) pike, carp, porgy or
        sea bass
  ¹/₄ cup Spanish olive oil
  ¹/₄ cup melted butter
     2 tablespoons soy sauce
     2 tablespoons lemon juice
     1 tablespoons crushed hot red pepper
  ¹/₂ teaspoons salt
  ¹/₄ teaspoon coarsely ground black pepper
     3 cups cooked rice

Clean and rinse fish; pat dry with paper towels. Make several diagonal slashes on each side and place in ovenproof dish. Mix remaining ingredients and pour over fish. Bake at 350°F. for about 30 minutes, basting several times, or until fish is done and flakes easily with fork. Serve with hot fluffy rice. Makes 6 servings.

```
CALORIES PER SERVING ............................ 305
GRAMS OF PROTEIN PER SERVING ................... 17
GRAMS OF CARBOHYDRATE PER SERVING ........... 18
GRAMS OF FAT PER SERVING ........................ 17
```

Mock Sukiyaki
(Japan)

     1 pound round steak (³/₄-in. thick)
  1¹/₂ cups diagonally sliced celery
  1¹/₂ cups sliced fresh mushrooms (about ¹/₄ lb.)
  ¹/₂ cup green onion cut in 2-inch pieces
     2 tablespoons Spanish olive oil
     1 can (10¹/₂ oz.) beef gravy
  ¹/₂ pound fresh spinach, torn in bite-size
        pieces (about 6 cups)
     2 tablespoons soy sauce
     2 cups cooked rice

Freeze meat 1 hour to firm (makes slicing easier); slice into very thin strips. In skillet, saute celery, mushrooms and onion in olive oil until just tender; push to one side. Add meat; cook briefly until color changes. Add gravy, spinach, soy sauce. Heat; stir occasionally. Serve with rice. Makes 4 servings.

```
CALORIES PER SERVING ............................ 637
GRAMS OF PROTEIN PER SERVING ................... 41
GRAMS OF CARBOHYDRATE PER SERVING ........... 32
GRAMS OF FAT PER SERVING ........................ 37
```

Index

The American Way... with Olive Oil